Mixed Realism

Electronic Mediations

SERIES EDITORS: N. KATHERINE HAYLES, PETER KRAPP, RITA RALEY, AND SAMUEL WEBER

FOUNDING EDITOR: MARK POSTER

(*continued on page 207*)

Mixed Realism

Videogames and the Violence of Fiction

TIMOTHY J. WELSH

Electronic Mediations 50

UNIVERSITY OF MINNESOTA PRESS

MINNEAPOLIS • LONDON

An earlier version of chapter 7 was published as "Face to Face: Humanizing the Digital Display in *Call of Duty: Modern Warfare 2*," in *Guns, Grenades, and Grunts: First-Person Shooter Games,* ed. Gerald Voorhees, Josh Call, and Katie Whitlock, 389–414 (London: Continuum, 2012).

Published by the University of Minnesota Press
111 Third Avenue South, Suite 290
Minneapolis, MN 55401-2520
http://www.upress.umn.edu

A Cataloging-in-Publication record for this book is available from the Library of Congress.
ISBN: 978-0-8166-8943-9 (hc)
ISBN: 978-0-8166-9608-6 (pb)

Printed in the United States of America on acid-free paper

The University of Minnesota is an equal-opportunity educator and employer.

21 20 19 18 17 16   10 9 8 7 6 5 4 3 2 1

CONTENTS

PREFACE

Fair warning: to paraphrase Johnny Truant in *House of Leaves*, this book may not be for you. Part of the issue has to do with its scope and methodology, the other part has to do with what that methodology implies, its stakes and consequences.

Some background first. When I started out, I thought I was writing a book about the inadequacy of immersion metaphors to describe the role of media-generated virtualities in everyday life. As a videogame scholar and longtime player, I was—and still am—frustrated by the continued use of these metaphors in the marketing and criticism of videogames and digital media more generally. It struck me that the much of the anxiety and excitement surrounding videogames hinged on an expectation that when playing I somehow didn't know what I was doing, that it was possible to lose track of the fact that the projections on-screen were only virtual. I wanted to come up with a critical approach that gave players a little more credit.

As a literary scholar, I understood the immersion metaphors as proceeding from and depending on prior assumptions about reading. I recognized that similar anxieties previously circulated around fiction in print. Furthermore, during the same period that videogames developed as a dominant industry, literary fiction and literary theorists actively tried to upset the immersiveness of fiction and impose different reading practices. My plan was to juxtapose videogames with some of these print literature contemporaries.

Doing so would hopefully reveal the internal contradictions in the concept of immersion that got mapped on to digital technologies in the 1990s and persists today. What I found, though, was that these virtualities kept folding back on me.

The fictions I chose to work with were ones that in some way included my act of being audience to them as part of their conceit. *House of Leaves*, for example, is a novel that presents itself as book of film criticism and so presumes being read; or, on the videogame side, *.hack//Infection* is a videogame in which the player's character plays videogames. These examples demonstrated to me the possibility of self-conscious immersion, where I enter into the fiction despite and, in fact, through my awareness of my own mediated engagement. But, even as these fictions absorbed my self-aware interaction, they couldn't or didn't dislodge it from the lived contexts in which it took place. Like a Möbius strip, the interior was also the exterior which was at the same time inside. It all seemed very convoluted.

The capacity these texts exhibited to fold their fictions back on me as a media user isn't really about representation. Of course they described things that had recognizable real-world counterparts. Beyond that, they require real-world actions. Not in the Columbine theory sense of influencing players to be violent, because the action they provoked was merely their own use, was the playing of a videogame, the reading of a novel. All of a sudden, these supposedly discrete virtual worlds were staging real-world events. Furthermore, because of the expanded role of virtuality in the everyday life of wired culture, it seemed to me that the supposedly banal activities these fictions provoked were charged with meaning, significance, and opportunity.

I started using the term "mixed realism" to describe how the virtual reframes the active task of engaging it within other material contexts and circumstances. It seems to me that this is a necessary function of fiction: to enter a banal activity—like pressing buttons on a controller or turning the pages of a book—within more crucial contexts. To see this operation of reframing in action, though, to engage with media with an awareness of this happening, requires a different sort of reading practice.

I'm using "reading" here as shorthand for the kind of attentive audienceship that describes how one consumes a novel, watches a movie, plays a videogame, or uses media in the broadest sense. It is not intended to give undue preference to the print or the literary. At it turns out, coming up with a term adequate to these different but related media activities can be quite difficult. This is part of the difficulty of this book.

Virtuality enters our lives through all sorts of devices—phones, computers, televisions, games consoles, ATMs, in-dash monitors, et cetera—each with a set of affordances and attendant cultural practices. Each platform requires its own kind of user interactions and, in turn, rightly demands its own media-specific analysis and critical engagement. In short, every instance of media use theoretically prompts its own version of mixed realism. If we are to understand how media-generated virtualities participate in daily life, all of these domains, practices, media objects, and affordances are relevant. We need ways to speak across them all—a trànsmedia methodology—while attending to material specificities of each instantiation, each embodiment as N. Katherine Hayles would say.

My project, then, is fundamentally interdisciplinary and, lamentably, unavoidably insufficient. There are quite simply too many sites, too many media, too many practices participating in or enacting mixed realism in their own ways for me to address here without gross generalizations and oversimplifications. To cope with this, the present volume focuses on two media forms: videogames and print literature. I selected these two for a couple of reasons. They are (1) frequently considered to be at odds, competitors for influence on culture, though they (2) both participate in similar assumptions about how media works and how it absorbs its audience. Further, both media forms (3) seem, or are often assumed to be, self-contained, offering discrete fictional environments.

As a result, the games and novels I present here offer challenging test cases to unpack. If I can show how media as divergent as serious print literature and mass-market console videogames both participate in mixed realism, I will have powerful models for how to look for mixed realism in other sites. If I do my job well, if you find this a compelling way to look at the fictional in wired culture, hopefully you will extend this work and chart the circuits of interaction spreading out through other media, other performances, other sites of virtuality.

This leads to the second reason this book might not be for you. Learning to see this way can be uncomfortable because it opens up and pours on our heads more responsibility and agency than we typically want from our media. All those seemingly innocuous fictions become suddenly active, reconfiguring the practices of daily life, involving you in distant and diverse real-world contexts. Even as you take up and read this very book, mixed realism circulates in ways I couldn't possibly imagine, much less address here. The activation of these circuits depends on and flows through you, dear reader. Once you have the right orientation toward virtuality, you'll begin to see mixed realism everywhere, from your computer's operating system to the branding on your single-serving coffee pod.

Or perhaps you won't. Maybe you will, as Johnny Truant recommends regarding his treacherous book, dismiss the whole enterprise of mixed realism out of hand. If so, I hope that in the very least this book will convince you to take to heart the fundamental issue that motivates it.

As media and the virtualities they generate continue to proliferate, infiltrating and mediating ever more processes of daily life in wired culture, the models we use to discuss them cannot continue to divide up reality. We need approaches to media and mediation broadly conceived that seek to recover virtuality as a domain of actual lived experience, or else we will undermine, obscure, and overlook the very modality of wired culture. Even if mixed realism is not for you, if it doesn't grant the awareness and agency to navigate the weird, outpostless overlappings of material and virtual contexts that make up our mixed reality, we need something that can.

The Paradox of Real Virtuality

Super Columbine Massacre RPG!

The proliferation of digital communication technologies has made interactions within virtual environments an ordinary occurrence. At this advanced stage of wired culture, our interactions with media-generated virtuality are exceedingly banal. We make balance transfers at an ATM, update Facebook timelines, and squeeze in sessions of *Angry Birds* (Rovio, 2009) on the subway. The virtual environments at play in these scenarios certainly do not threaten our grasp on "reality," and each has very real and recognizable economic, social, and cultural effects. Cyberspace is "everting," as William Gibson puts it, turned inside out and integrated everywhere (everyware?) and in everything.[1] Attempting to isolate the virtually real from the really real—as if it were possible—risks obscuring interactions that crisscross presumed ontological boundaries. Wired culture is a mixed reality, conducted as exchanges between virtual and material contexts.

Even so, the virtual is still frequently figured as "false, illusory, or imaginary."[2] This characterization is a holdover from "science fictions" circulated during the mid-1990s,[3] which retroactively positioned Gibson's hallucinatory cyberspace as origin and endpoint for "a future in which people could 'step into' their computers rather than look at them, and how different everything would be when that happened."[4] The forecasts of cyberpunk writers and the prophets of virtual reality never materialized, nor did they accurately represent a typical user's relationship to virtuality. Yet the vision of wholly immersive media set the virtualities of digital technology in opposition to "reality," even as the increased affordability of personal computers, the spread of Internet connectivity, and a fifth generation of videogame consoles made them a part of everyday life.

The immersive fallacy is neither originally nor primarily digital. When the printing press was a new media, Cervantes's *Don Quixote* addressed the fear that romances might play havoc with the mind of a susceptible reader. Realist authors of the nineteenth century "felt a mission to displace fiction that inspired destructive fantasy" by aspiring to "objective" representations of real life that might inspire social reforms.[5] Over a century later, their style came to be regarded as the very model of immersive literature, print media's closest equivalent to the projections of virtual reality simulation technologies.[6] Meanwhile, the literature of the post-WWII period—that tracked with the development of those VR technologies and saw Vannevar Bush's outline of a memex realized in the now ubiquitous Web—would be identified by a preoccupation with shifting ontological boundaries.[7] Its characteristic self-reflexivity frustrates immersive access by drawing attention to artifice.[8] Ironically, when prompting readers to acknowledge media and mediation modern life, these metafictions are at their most realistic.

The unshakeable anxiety about immersive media has passed on to videogames. Often placed in competition with print literature, videogames have inherited many of the same investments in questions of mediation, representation, and responsibility and updating them for a digital age. The recurring public discussion of videogames oscillates between excitement and fear that gamers might not be able to tell the difference between the virtual and real. Yet the more pressing question may be how these fictional environments reveal and facilitate transactions between supposedly separate domains.

The peculiarities of the condition of virtuality today are best understood through the particularities of specific instantiations. Let us open the discussion, then, with several vignettes of pubic discourse on virtuality and its relationship to reality.

Super Columbine Massacre RPG!

Danny Ledonne's *Super Columbine Massacre RPG!* received little public attention when it first appeared online as a free download in April 2005. The "electronic documentary," as Ledonne calls it, places players in the role of gunmen Eric Harris and Dylan Klebold as they prepare and conduct their assault on Columbine High School.[9] Having felt ostracized as a Colorado teenager himself, Ledonne took special interest in the Columbine shooting and conducted extensive research on the shooters, their written and video diaries, the events leading up to and during April 20, 1999, and the subsequent media treatment. In an artist's statement published with *Super Columbine Massacre RPG!* Ledonne explains that he intended the game to "[push] the envelope as to what a video game can be."[10] Often "relegated to escapist entertainment," the videogame medium is significantly lacking "in the realm of socially conscious gaming—software that does more than merely amuse for a few idle hours." *Super Columbine Massacre RPG!* represents an attempt to "make something that mattered" as opposed to "an easily forgotten adventure set in a mythical realm of dragons or spaceships." In other words, Ledonne identifies the problem with videogames as their failure to bridge the gap between on-screen virtualities and off-screen realities.

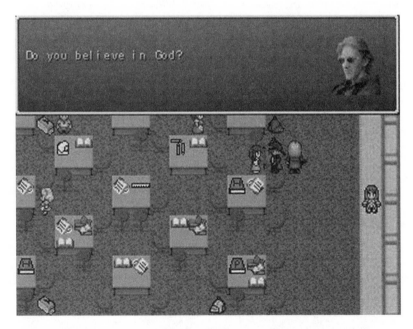

FIGURE I.1. Screenshot from Danny Ledonne's *Super Columbine Massacre RPG!* depicting one of the more famous moments from the attack on Columbine High School.

To solve this problem, Ledonne decided to make the "unthinkable game," a videogame depicting a real school shooting frequently blamed on the influence of violent videogames. Many in both the media and the psychiatric community attributed at least some portion of what happened at Columbine to the fact that Harris and Klebold were "immersed" in first-person shooters like *Doom* (id Software, 1993).[11] With this as a cultural context, Ledonne intended his violent game to spark discussion about actual violence "beyond the simple platitudes and panaceas of gun control, media ratings/censorship, bully prevention programs, and parental supervision." Unfortunately that was not how the game entered the public conversation.

The polarizing debate Ledonne sought out began nearly a year after the game's release. In May 2006 Ian Bogost wrote about *Super Columbine Massacre RPG!* for the website *Water Cooler Games*, calling it "brave, sophisticated, and worthy of praise from those of us interested in videogames with an agenda."[12] Soon after, the Associated Press brought national exposure to *Super Columbine Massacre RPG!* when it picked up an interview with Bogost in which he discussed the "culture of ineffability" surrounding the game.[13] A torrent of "largely reactionary" media coverage followed.[14] Emru Townsend of *PC World*, for example, called the game "appalling" and ranked it the second-worst videogame of all time, one spot higher on the list than a game whose object is to repeatedly rape a Native American woman.[15] The Dawson College shooting later that year stoked the outcry against the game, and Ledonne was frequently called on to answer for the influence his game may or may not have had on the gunman, Kimveer Gill. The public discussion of *Super Columbine Massacre RPG!* culminated in 2007 when festival organizers pulled the game from the Slamdance Film Festival's "Guerrilla Gamemaker Competition," citing a "moral obligation" raised by "this particular game."[16] Six of the finalists—including renowned independent developers Jonathan Blow, Kellee Santiago, and The Behemoth—withdrew from the competition in protest.

That controversy attends a videogame in which players act out a school shooting comes as no surprise. What is interesting for my purposes here is how debates such as these—ostensibly about violence in the media—consistently return to the question of "realism."

Objections to Ledonne's "electronic documentary" typically took one of two forms. On the one hand, those like Brian Rohrbough's, whose son,

Daniel, was killed at Columbine, were offended that an actual mass murder could be played like a game: "It disgusts me. You trivialize the actions of two murderers and the lives of the innocent."[17] On the other hand, opponents voiced concerns that players might become immersed in *Super Columbine Massacre RPG!* the way Harris and Klebold were immersed in *Doom*. In the aftermath of the Dawson College shooting, it was widely reported that Gill both admired the Columbine shooters and was an avid fan of *Super Columbine Massacre RPG!*[18] For many, Gill confirmed the belief that the virtual violence of videogames—*Super Columbine Massacre RPG!* included—inspires actual violence. As the antiviolence advocate Val Smith put it, "For [Ledonne] to believe that you can put a game out into the public domain and expect that no one will be influenced is naive at best and possibly criminally negligent."[19]

These two common objections to *Super Columbine Massacre RPG!* share an imperative to distinguish and separate virtual violence from "real" violence. Taken together, though, these accusations characterize *Super Columbine Massacre RPG!* as somehow simultaneously inadequate to the tragic shooting at Columbine and yet so compelling that it instigated the shooting at Dawson. In other words, *Super Columbine Massacre RPG!* is at the same time too unrealistic and too realistic.

This is the paradox of real virtuality. We know very well that the media-generated virtualities that fill our lives are not what they represent; as Jesper Juul put it, the dragon on screen is not a *real* dragon.[20] But these virtualities are *something*. The virtual environments of digital media play a variety of roles in contemporary culture, mediating all manner of daily activity. We have grown familiar with these technologies, comfortable with making interactions in and with nonphysical environments. Yet these generated "worlds" remain somehow less than real, somehow in competition with the physical world.

How do we account for media-generated virtualities in real life? Do they have presence, significance, or influence exceeding their material instantiations and user processes that invoke them? What of the virtualities themselves? What relationships do they establish through and beyond our interactions with them?

Questions like these may sound outdated, like a return to the cyber-hype we gladly left behind in the late 1990s. Indeed, this book's response to them will require returning to the dot-com era and undoing assumptions about digital virtualities ingrained then in order to outline a new model. But it is essential to return to these issues, even at this late date when wired culture becomes increasingly wireless, because the paradox of real virtuality continues to structure our relationship with digitally generated environments.

Newtown

This book was under review on December 14, 2012, the day Adam Lanza walked into Sandy Hook Elementary School and fatally shot twenty children and six adults. Later that day, President Barack Obama paused to wipe away tears as he addressed the nation, saying, "We're going to have to come together and take meaningful action to prevent more tragedies like this, regardless of the politics."[21] The events in Newtown thrust the issue of gun violence into the forefront of the public consciousness, sparking vigorous and much-needed debate about America's relationship with guns. And, as it did following Columbine in 1999, violence and videogames featured prominently in these discussions.

Though it may have been *more* unusual for the college-aged Lanza to have had no interest in videogames,[22] once it was discovered that the shooter enjoyed everything from *Call of Duty: Modern Warfare 2* (Infinity Ward, 2009) to *Dynasty Warriors* (Omega Force, 1997), videogames were immediately implicated in the tragedy.[23] Four days after his tearful address, Obama announced that Vice President Joe Biden would lead a task force charged with providing recommendations on reducing gun violence.[24] Though Obama focused on stricter gun regulations—specifically suggesting a ban on "weapons of war" like assault rifles—Biden's team addressed a "broad range of ideas," which, of course, included violent videogames. On January 10, 2013, Biden met with the National Rifle Association and, on January 11, 2013, with the Entertainment Software Association.[25] In effect, the task force discussed "real" guns one day and "virtual" guns the next.

Brown v. Electronic Merchants Association

Despite the near ubiquity of virtual environments in wired culture, despite videogaming's casual revolution, public discussion of violence and videogames still presumes compatibility between on-screen representations and off-screen realities. Indeed, the same conflation of virtual and real under-girded the state of California's oral arguments a little more than three years prior to Biden's consortium. In *Brown v. Electronic Merchants Association* the Supreme Court heard arguments from the state of California for the right to impose tighter restrictions on the sale of violent videogames to minors. Arguing that violent games require restrictions not leveed on books, cartoons, movies, and other entertainment media, California Deputy Attorney General Zackery Morazzini explained that the "interactive nature of violent [games]," in which the player is "acting out this—this obscene level of violence," makes gaming "especially harmful to minors."[26] He then suggested that the obscenity of an individual game could be determined by viewing "video clips of game play," effectively removing interactivity from consideration.

Later on, Chief Justice John Roberts argued in support of Morazzini, stating that "in these video games the child is not sitting there passively watching something; the child is doing the killing. The child is doing the maiming."[27] The Court, in such statements, asserts compatibility between on-screen representations and the off-screen violence. The player's real-world interaction with the media—the physical actions the player undertakes to initiate those on-screen representations—drops out, collapsed into their off-screen analogues.

Project Natal

Even though such public policy discussions are rarely about videogames, one would hope that Biden's summit would benefit from having representatives from the videogame industry there to advance a more sophisticated discussion of interactivity.[28] Yet the videogame industry itself often reproduces the same uneasy conflation of action and representation. Videogame companies consistently market their products as so intuitive and immersive that they overcome the burden of interface. In other words, videogames are sold on still-prevalent assumptions about the immersivity of virtual environments.

During the Microsoft press event at the 2009 Electronic Entertainment Expo (E3), Peter Molyneux—then the creative director of Microsoft Game Studios, Europe—introduced Project Natal, the Xbox 360's controller-less interface device now known as Kinect. Molyneux, in grandiose style, opened

FIGURE I.2. Demonstration of human interaction with Lionhead Studios' *Milo*, a tech demo of the Microsoft Kinect (formerly Project Natal) platform, presented at E3 in 2009. Here, Clare attempts to put her hands in a virtual pond.

by positing that the controller—"that thing in our hands," as he put it— prevents the creation of truly interactive games. He then showed a video in which a woman named Clare engaged with the virtual world of a boy named Milo by gesturing in front of Natal as Molyneux cooed, "There Clare is, in Milo's world. She's in that pond."[29]

No matter how "intuitive" or "natural" gesture controls become, devices like Natal merely swap one interface for another, one mode of interactivity for another. Yet, even on the leading edge of commercial gaming technology, the industry describes its products and aims no differently than the heralds of first-generation virtual reality in the mid-1990s. Back then, Project Natal might have been said to have the potential for the "virtual reality effect," the "denial of the role of hardware and software (bits, pixels, and binary code) in the production of what the user experiences as unmediated presence."[30] She's in that pond!

The Techno-materialist Turn

These examples reveal persistent, problematic assumptions about the re- lationship between the virtual and the real, assumptions that continue to structure discourse surrounding digital media even today. Contemporary scholars of digital media will recognize in these examples an underlying immersive fallacy, the belief that eventually the technology will advance to the point that frame falls away and it becomes invisible. After fifteen years of technological development, daily use, and sophisticated study and theorization of digital virtuality's role in modern culture, one would think that we had overcome such notions. As Justice Roberts and Molyneux demonstrate—and the debates surrounding *Super Columbine Massacre RPG!* and Newtown affirm—the immersive fallacy is alive and well in both debates about public policy and the marketing of new technologies.[31] Whereas Molyneux forecasts that new developments in interface will erase the boundary between act and representation, from the Court's perspective we are already there. No matter what the player is actually doing—whether it is pressing buttons or gesturing to a camera—her engagement with the interface, hardware, and platform is immaterial. The goal of interaction is to disappear in service of immersion.

At least the last fifteen years of digital media studies has sought to dispel such immersive fallacies by asserting the primacy of the material properties and uses of digital media. Following N. Katherine Hayles's call during the dot-com boom to rebalance the information/materiality binary,[32] the techno-materialist turn brought intelligent and insightful discussions about the physical qualities of media, the embodied experiences of users, and the conditions of production. However, while these works offer important correctives to mainstream debates, they too often confirm and reinscribe the same ontological division between the virtual and the real. While figures like Justice Roberts and Molyneux expect the allure of virtual environments to absorb the operation of hardware, techno-materialists push too far in the opposite direction. Even Hayles herself now receives criticism for being insufficiently materialist in her terminology.[33] As I will discuss in chapter 3, such "short-sighted essentialisms," whereby virtuality is frequently undermined in favor of some "more real" component layer, are particularly prevalent in the study of videogames.[34]

Even as digital technologies take on ever-greater influence in the wired world, the virtual/real binary continues to structure our interactions with them. Commercial technologies have never (and will never) make good on the promise of immersion; and yet they are still marketed, debated, and legislated in those terms. All the while, scholars of digital media have made every effort to make these technologies more visible. In doing so, virtuality itself has become secondary, derivative, or optional and its participation in wired culture obscured. The binary intact, the virtual remains a realm of escapism and fantastic diversion, leaving little response to the more "vapory" aspects of digital media—like the role of virtual violence in contemporary culture.[35]

The Complicated Realism of *Super Columbine Massacre RPG!*

To begin to explore this role, let us return to Ledonne's "electronic documentary." Careful consideration of the game's engagement with its source material reveals a relationship quite different from and more extensive than representation. The suggestion that the pixelated on-screen virtualities of *Super Columbine Massacre RPG!* might be confused with the off-screen events they depict is difficult to fathom. Lacking experience as a programmer,

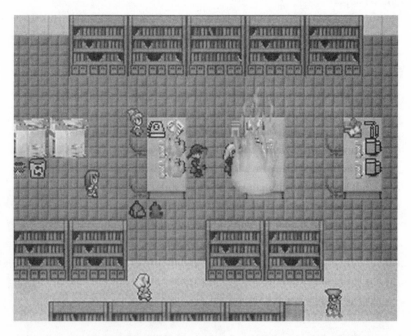

FIGURE 1.3. Harris and Klebold blow up the computers in the school library in Danny Ledonne's *Super Columbine Massacre RPG!*

Ledonne produced the game using ASCII's *RPG Maker 2000*, which allows users with limited design skills to piece together simple, 8-bit games from templates, sample graphics, and scripted mechanics. The result is an amateurish and cartoony game that would have appeared at least twelve years out of date even at the time of the shooting.

Contrary to expectation, the game is not a first-person shooter (FPS) but a menu-driven role-playing game (RPG) in the style of *Final Fantasy* (Square, 1987). Players move Harris and Klebold freely through blocky, two-dimensional environments representing the school grounds, hallways, and classrooms. Lethal encounters with non-playable characters (NPCs)— the shooters' classmates and teachers—are translated into text-based menu selections. Moreover, about halfway through, the game shifts away from fact-based, interactive New Journalism and follows Harris and Klebold into hell, where they take on monsters from *Doom* and chat with pop-culture icons.

Super Columbine Massacre RPG! portrays the tragedy at Columbine in an abstract, highly mediated fashion. It is based on extensive research about an

FIGURE I.4. Combat menu from Danny Ledonne's *Super Columbine Massacre RPG!*

actual event, but neither the graphics nor the gameplay approach realistic depiction and the second half of the game shifts abruptly into surrealism and parody. Yet, even as it foregoes representational fidelity, *Super Columbine Massacre RPG!* still takes on an eerie presence and a disconcerting realism. Patrick Dugan describes this quality of the game when he suggests that the "public's aversion" to *Super Columbine Massacre RPG!* had less to do with the game's content than with the proximity to the actual events it imposes on players: "A 'respectable' medium like film or literature imply a greater degree of removal of the audience from the subject matter, but a game is frighteningly visceral, and according to critics, 'too interactive'—which is kind of like saying a film is 'too lit' or a book is 'too wordy.'"[36] Interactivity is certainly a fundamental property of the videogame medium, as essential to its representative capacities as light is to movies and words are to novels. But the larger issue Dugan's comment raises is not that the game is "too interactive" but somehow too *close* to the real event. Indeed, what makes *Super Columbine Massacre RPG!* so "frighteningly visceral" is that to play the game is itself a kind of interaction with the actual Columbine shooting.

The *Washington Post* technology columnist Mike Musgrove reported having this experience when trying to play *Super Columbine Massacre RPG!*[37] Despite having eliminated innumerable NPCs in his videogaming past, he found he could not bring himself to direct Harris and Klebold to fire on their classmates. Musgrove comments that he "didn't want to be responsible for the real-world violence that happened that day, even in a game." Indeed, the player's enactment of the Columbine shooting in a virtual environment occupies the same historical reality as the actual shooting. In this sense, *Super Columbine Massacre RPG!* removes the screen between representation and reality and between players and the tragic event. That proximity produces the kind of experience Musgrove describes, this sense that his virtual killing is somehow implicated in real deaths.

But what is the nature or extent of this implication? How could interacting with a virtual space be implicated in historical events? How could playing a digital game about killing be involved in killing? How does this virtuality participate in reality?

Had he continued, Musgrove would have found how banal and tedious the in-game slaying turns out to be. After clearing a few rooms, I found the turn-based, menu-driven combat system increasingly repetitive, seemingly pointless, and eventually tiresome. None of the unarmed school inhabitants posed any threat or challenge to my Harris and Klebold, and soon there appeared to be no reason to continue with the shooting spree. Killing classmates became *boring*.

In effect, the design of *Super Columbine Massacre RPG!* desensitizes players to the on-screen violence. It could thereby be said to implicate players in same affect attributed to Harris and Klebold as fans of violent media. At the same time, however, the game consistently complicates assumptions about how Harris and Klebold came to the point of shooting up their school. The inclusion of direct quotations from the gunmen's journals, video recordings, and suicide tape along with flashback cut scenes of life at Columbine before the shooting reference Harris and Klebold as historical figures. Though I play from the shooters' perspective, allusions to their real lived experiences differentiate playable avatars from the living people they represent. In turn, these references draw attention to gameplay as a mediated experience. Thus the complex of experience and emotion that led Harris and Klebold to open fire on their classmates is irrevocably distinguished from my dispassionate act of making some menu selections in coordination with an on-screen display.

Even so, by playing the game, the player has been exposed to a piece of violent media, and one that specifically has been implicated in real killing. The shootings at Dawson College demonstrated in tragic fashion that *Super Columbine Massacre RPG!* carries its own risks. Yet they are risks taken on the confident claim that such tragedies cannot be attributed to a single factor or influence like gun control, bullying, or violent media. To make this claim, *Super Columbine Massacre RPG!*, as a piece of violent media about violence supposedly caused by media, folds back on its players.

The game subjects its players to virtual violence and, by extension, all the social, political, and ethical consequences that surround it. Whatever my reaction to the school shooting in the first half of *Super Columbine Massacre RPG!*, by playing through it I become an active participant within the same violent media ecology as Harris, Klebold, Gill, and innumerable other "troubled" gamers. As it transitions into the second stage, set in hell, the game demonstrates how the stakes that attend my position as gamer belong to an entire social milieu.

Throughout the game, but particularly during the hell level, *Super Columbine Massacre RPG!* situates the events at Columbine in relation to a set of complex and deep-seated cultural attitudes toward violence. Harris and Klebold's descent into the afterlife recalls similar episodes in Homer and Dante, thereby positioning videogames in a lineage of violent media that goes back to the foundations of Western literary culture. As the two shooters discuss the nature of judgment with philosophers, politicians, scientists, celebrities, and fictional characters, it becomes clear that *Super Columbine Massacre RPG!* has adopted the grammar of violent media to expose and critique these inherited cultural attitudes from the inside.[38]

The difficulty ramps up significantly once players reach the hell level. Having forgone the experience points I could have earned by tediously blasting through unarmed classmates and teachers, my Harris and Klebold prove somewhat underpowered against the demons and zombie space marines from *Doom*, the icons of their supposed desensitization. The use of conventional tropes and game mechanics to tell the shooters' story plays out as

FIGURE I.5. Iconic enemies from *Doom* attack Harris and Klebold in the hell level of Danny Ledonne's *Super Columbine Massacre RPG!*

a sardonic parody of "the power fantasy ... represented in at least 90% of games on the market."[39] As I subject Harris and Klebold to a gauntlet of popular violent media, *Super Columbine Massacre RPG!* makes intimations about my own participation in the culture of violence with which the shooters struggled to overcome, both virtually on-screen and in their tragic off-screen lives. I am here implicated in the Columbine shooting, not as a fellow killer but as a fellow consumer. Playing *Super Columbine Massacre RPG!* is to play at one's position as media user within a culture steeped in violence and in turn acknowledge responsibility, as participants within this milieu, for the "real-world violence that happened that day."

Of course, this is not the kind of "realism" that disturbs videogaming's detractors. Despite accusations to the contrary, *Super Columbine Massacre RPG!* cannot support the kind of immersive experience that is simultaneously a major selling point of contemporary games and a core concern for policy makers and parents. It cannot transport players to another place and time, put them "in the shoes" of the killers, or give them the experience of "real" violence, because, at every turn, its out-of-date graphics, menu-driven action, and self-referential dialogue remind players that this is a just videogame. Yet we play this violent videogame in the same "real world" that Harris and Klebold played *Doom* and killed thirteen teachers and classmates. With this recognition, Ledonne's fictionalized retelling starts to feel too close to actual events and its on-screen virtualities become frighteningly visceral.

Quite beyond their capacity for verisimilitude, media-generated virtualities themselves participate in the lives of their users. These virtual worlds and virtual objects have relationships with and significance within real-world contexts. When we interact with them, they have the capacity to position us within seemingly disparate social and material realities. When I select a pipe bomb to lob at pixelated classmates in *Super Columbine Massacre RPG!* I am interacting with the broader culture of violence, for example. Even though, with its blocky, 8-bit graphics and menu-driven action, the game forgoes representational realism, it manages to join the player's engagements with insignificant, infinitely respawnable virtual objects to the "real-world violence that happened that day." On-screen and off-screen contexts overlap as actions in a virtual world take on simultaneous agency in the real one.

Mixed Realism

Super Columbine Massacre RPG! exemplifies what I am calling *mixed realism*. Mixed realism describes the ways media-generated virtualities reframe or recontextualize the real-world activity of interacting with them. Rather than a particular aesthetic style or technical paradigm, it refers to the capacity for virtual environments and virtual objects to situate their users within social, material, and ethical contexts.

The proliferation of digital communication technologies into all aspects of modern life in the wired world has inserted interactions with and in virtual environments into all manner of social practice. Seemingly disparate activities and social spheres come in contact through their shared participation in a media ecology. These media-generated environments and objects have the capacity to not only expose these relationships but also facilitate exchanges between them.

Mixed realism, in this sense, is a particular kind of what Robert Mitchell calls "folding." Mitchell uses the term to describe how the incorporation of real biological material into works of bioart folds together the milieus of the art world and the biotech industry, enabling "new constellations of things, people and institutions."[40] Beatriz da Costa's *Transgenic Bacteria Release Machine*, for instance, brings real, though completely harmless, transgenic bacteria into the gallery space, literally exposing patrons to the products of commercialized bio-matter.[41] In the case of mixed realism, instead of real biological material, it is the real media-generated virtualities that occupy a crease point where the seemingly innocuous task of playing a videogame, using the Internet, or reading a book comes in contact with other social spaces and media practices.

Facebook, for example, ostensibly has nothing to do with agriculture. The popular Facebook virtual-farming game *FarmVille* (Zynga, 2009), however, draws on and extends the operation of Facebook, recontextualizing a database activity in relation to farming and the cultural understanding of farming. Playing *FarmVille* does not involve confusion about the boundary between a "real" farm and the one on-screen. Rather, by folding agriculture onto the activity of using Facebook, *FarmVille* reconfigures both. It exposes the ways that using Facebook relates to farming within wired culture. The seemingly simple act of managing virtual crops participates in the digitization of modern farm practices, the informatization of the food industry, meal cultures, and so on, as they mingle with the particular kinds of sociality and social practices afforded by digital interfaces with online databases and communication networks.

Because mixed realism focuses on the correspondences between virtualities and the lived contexts in which we engage them, it inherently attends to media specificity while also remaining applicable to a variety of media platforms. Print fiction, for instance, generates its own kind of media-dependent virtual environment, and so demonstrates a capacity for mixed realism. For example, the title of David Foster Wallace's 1996 magnum opus, *Infinite Jest*, establishes a feedback loop between the reader's act of reading the novel and the fictional story revolving around a film cartridge also titled *Infinite Jest*, a video so compelling that its viewers become catatonic.[42] This small gesture of self-reference creates a hinge where the central issues motivating the world of the novel fold back onto the task of reading. The title wavers between arrogance and self-deprecation. It declares that the novel at hand is the most compelling entertainment of all time. Failing to achieve "infinite jest," the novel winds up being really long. Sending the reader back and forth, tediously, between the central text and one-hundred-plus pages of endnotes becomes its own seemingly unending joke. Instead of paralyzing pleasure, the novel risks the boredom, disappointment, and disaffection with which the story grapples.

The promise of mixed realism is that it can help us understand the vast variety of relationships that virtualities forge between and within different real-world contexts. It can describe how during the Arab Spring protesters used social media sites like Twitter to augment a restricted and dangerous physical environment with the virtual one of update timelines. With most communication networks shut down, these timelines mediated events on the ground in close-to-real time, giving the protests the form of numerous, fragmented, simultaneous, interweaving narratives for most of the outside world. The consumption of and interaction with (in the form of supportive replies and retweets) the online protests became a significant form of participation even for those who were not physically present. In turn, this participation reconstituted the Arab Spring as a social media revolution, even in some cases overshadowing the protests themselves with renewed—problematic—discussions of social media as a liberatory platform.[43]

On a more mundane level, mixed realism describes the simulated leather of Apple's iCal application as it connects on-screen and off-screen workspaces. Even as Microsoft attempted to get away from such literal skeuomorphic design metaphors with its recent Metro interface style, it wound up establishing a similar circuitry of interaction. Inspired by way-finding graphics in public transit systems—such as Seattle's King County Metro—the Metro interface was designed for touch-screen mobile devices like smartphones and tablet computers.[44] As a result, today's immaterial laborers can maintain 24/7 connectivity with the workplace within the same graphic environment as they travel to and from their physical office on the bus or subway, their mobile office.

Mixed realism gives a name to these and innumerable other scenarios in which virtuality has everted and become integrated with our lived environments. In fact, the flexibility of mixed realism, its breadth of possible applications, means that the study that follows should in no way be considered comprehensive. Mixed realism circulates a little differently in each and every configuration, sometimes turning on a unique interaction or specific media affordance, a particular virtual object's appearance or behavior, or all of the above. For this reason, reading mixed realism is a process of careful tracing, following sometimes a singular aspect of the virtual as it reframes entirely our engagement with it by situating us within the broader media ecology. Further, each media object and each virtuality might accomplish this in varying and potentially competing ways as different aspects resonate across different areas of social life. As a result, any study of mixed realism—as I'm understanding the concept—has to proceed from examples and will be inevitably too specific, too narrow, and too close.

The present exploration has been restricted to single-player, major-release videogames and print literature, two particularly challenging modes of mixed realism. The characterization of videogames as immersive relies on and proceeds from prior assumptions about how readers get "lost" in a book. The gamble of this study is that presenting careful demonstrations of the mixed realism at play in exemplary videogames and print literature will show the way to applying the concept to a variety of implementation media that make up today's media ecology. Indeed, the persistence and common application of the immersion metaphor to such distinct media platforms indicates that current attitudes toward the virtual are symptomatic of long-held assumptions about media and mediation in general. Under a broad definition, all media-generated virtualities share the structure of an aesthetic object: form manifested in and through a medium. The well-established tradition of literary practice and criticism grappling with the relationship between art and life thus has special relevance to questions about the reality of the virtual attending contemporary digital technologies. In other words, the study of virtuality today requires a theory of fiction.

A New Relationship to Virtuality

If the twentieth century was about trying to recapture the real, as Alain Badiou has argued, then the twenty-first century will be about coming to terms with the virtual.[45] This book argues that doing so requires new models, ones that do not paradoxically oppose the virtual to the real. It seeks a different relationship to the virtual, one not bound by ontological hierarchies. It is about flows between on-screen and off-screen contexts. It is about the "mangle of play," "polyvalent doing," the "messiness" of virtual objects.[46] It is about player actions in virtual environments joining game systems to social systems, a circuit of interactivity. It is about fictions—both print and digital—integrated with the "processes of life."[47] It is about virtualities that complicate and extend beyond implementation media and our engagements with them. It is about the lessons of media-specific and material analysis revealing articulations of the formal and the fictional. It is about ontology giving way to aesthetics.

First, however, the vestiges of the mimetic binary—falsely dividing art from life and the virtual from the real—must be cleared away. For its part, this book seeks to unseat the still-prominent description of media-generated environments as "immersive," a metaphor that castes these virtualities as "a completely other reality."[48] The first section, comprising five chapters, presents targeted interventions at pivotal moments in the conception of virtual media through careful readings of the mixed realism of exemplary texts. Chapter 1 explains how first-generation virtual reality research and literary theory converged in the dot-com era to map an immersive binary onto media-generated virtualities. The second recovers a supposed ideally immersive literary text under that binary model, Truman Capote's 1966 nonfiction novel

In Cold Blood, laying the groundwork for a different relationship to virtuality through the perspective of mixed realism. Chapter 3 demonstrates how the techno-materialist turn near the end of the dot-com era—exemplified in the emerging field of videogame studies—maintains the virtual/real immersion binary even as it opposes the immersive fallacy. Then, in chapter 4, I present readings of three videogames, Ubisoft's *Prince of Persia: The Sands of Time* (2003), Silicon Knights's *Eternal Darkness: Sanity's Requiem* (Nintendo, 2002), and CyberConnect2's *.hack//Infection* (Bandai, 2002). For each of these examples from just after the dot-com crash, attention to mixed realism reveals how the incompleteness and incoherence of their virtual worlds facilitates exchanges with the digital milieu in which they are played. Chapter 5 offers a different point of intersection between digital technologies and print literature, comparing the burgeoning technical paradigm of mixed reality to the literary techniques of metafiction. In the process, it raises some of the lessons contemporary literature has to share about the hazards of a highly mediated culture.

The second section offers two extended studies in mixed realism, which explore the challenges and opportunities of living in an age of ubiquitous mediation. Chapter 6 deals with the threat Mark Danielewski's 2000 novel *House of Leaves* poses to its readers by drawing attention to pervasive and inescapable mediations of modern life. Chapter 7 treats Infinity Ward's *Call of Duty: Modern Warfare 2* (2009) as it positions its players within today's "virtuous war." Finally, the coda returns to media violence, comparing Rockstar's *Red Dead Redemption* (2010) to Cormac McCarthy's 1985 novel *Blood Meridian* in order to meditate on lingering questions of mixed realism.

The concept of mixed realism I am proposing attempts to deal with the weird, often-paradoxical ways media-generated virtualities participate in the everyday life of wired culture. The proliferation of digital media today makes urgent the recognition of how our interactions flow through these strange circuitries. To have any agency in the exchanges between virtual and "real" contexts requires first breaking the immersive binary that sets them in opposition.

I HISTORY, THEORY, METHODOLOGY

1 Immersive Fictions in the Dot-com Era

With a VR system you don't see the computer anymore—it's gone.

—JARON LANIER AND FRANK BIOCCA,
"An Insider's View of the Future of Virtual Reality"

The screen is gone.

—TOM WOLFE, *The New Journalism*

In *Becoming Virtual: Reality in the Digital Age*, published in 1998, Pierre Lévy clarifies that in terms of metaphysics "the virtual, strictly defined, has little relationship to that which is false, illusory, or imaginary."[1] To the contrary, he emphasizes that the virtual is a mode of being and "by no means the opposite of the real."[2] Even so, at the time he was writing, the suggestion that "reality in the digital age" was "becoming virtual" would likely strike many as something out of the film *The Matrix*, which would be released the following year.[3]

Lévy's book was published a year after the *Oxford English Dictionary Additions Series* amended the definition of "virtual" to include its general application to computer-generated environments, as in virtual reality (VR). In this application, "virtual" rarely takes on Lévy's strict metaphysical definition. Take, for instance, the definition of "virtual" provided by Theodor Nelson, which Howard Rheingold cites as foundational to the design philosophy of virtual reality technologies promoted during the dot-com era: "I use the term 'virtual' in its traditional sense, an opposite of 'real.' The *reality* of a movie includes how the scenery was painted and where the actors were repositioned between shots, but who cares? The *virtuality* of the movie is *what seems to be in it*. The *reality* of an interactive system includes its data structure and what language it's programmed in—but again, who cares?

The important concern is, *what does it seem to be?*"[4] In his early conceptualization of virtual reality technologies, Nelson places virtuality in opposition
to reality. The virtual here is in competition with the real—an immersive
binary—whereby the virtual intends to cover over its own implementation
and replace what "is" with what "seems to be."

The application of "virtual" to computer-generated environments—as
well as Lévy's call for redefinition—emerges during a period of intense popular interest surrounding digital technologies that arose concurrent with the
sharp increase in tech stock prices known as the dot-com bubble.[5] Though
conversations about the real and the virtual date back at least to Plato's Alle-
gory of the Cave, during the dot-com era they were undeniably mapped
on to the virtual environments of digital media.[6] Home Internet browsing
became commonplace, Web-based businesses succeeded (and failed), traditional companies moved online, and dedicated videogame consoles brought
3D virtual environments into the living room. As digital virtualities increasingly became everyday phenomena, they also came to be defined as the
opposite of "real."

Becoming Virtual is pitched specifically against this less-than-strict definition that was rapidly becoming the mainstream understanding of digitally mediated experiences. Telepresence technologies, online collaborative
media, cyberspace, and similar hallmarks of the digital age are for Lévy ideal
occasions to recognize the role of the virtual in contemporary society as "a
fecund and powerful mode of being that expands the process of creation,
opens up the future, injects a core of meaning beneath the platitude of immediate physical presence."[7] To interact with media-dependent virtualities in
this way, however, first requires unseating the expectation that they are "false,
illusory, or imaginary."

This chapter returns to the dot-com era in order to root out the immersive binary and clear the path to an alternative relationship to virtuality. To
do so, it will examine the intersection of the first-generation virtual reality
paradigm and literary theory during this period. The confluence of these
two fields reveals assumptions about virtuality and media more broadly, not
just on the leading edge of digital technology. Further, it opens an opportunity to confront the immersive binary by engaging traditional literary questions about the relationship between art and life, fact and fiction.

The Cutting Edge of Artificial Reality

No small portion of this alignment was due to the excitement about the potential implications advances in digital technologies might have for the future of immersive media. When tech stocks began to rise at the beginning of the dot-com era, interest swirled around developments in the first generation of virtual reality research. Edward Castronova writes, "In the early 1990s, as the dot-com hype was just beginning, technologist, novelists, pundits, and visionaries seemed to converge on the idea of VR as a transcendent technology of the immediate future."[8] More than just a hot investment opportunity, the prospect of fully immersive computer-generated environments—"the medium that tantalizes us"—captured the popular imagination as well.[9] Combined with the spread of Internet connectivity and remarkable improvements in videogame graphics, advancements in VR seemed to confirm that users would soon jack in to cyberspace. This was real technology that seemed to be approaching the experiences imagined by science fiction. "Although it sounds like science fiction, and the word 'cyberspace' in fact originated in a science-fiction novel," wrote Howard Rheingold, "virtual reality is already a science, a technology, and a business, supported by significant funding from the computer, communications, design, and entertainment industries worldwide."[10] A home version of the *Star Trek* holodeck couldn't be far off.

As innovations in VR were positioned as the future of technology, they were simultaneously figured as an evolution in the immersive experience of reading print fiction. "For centuries," Ron Wodaski writes in *Virtual Reality Madness!*, "books have been the cutting edge of artificial reality. Think about it: you read words on a page, and your mind fills in the pictures and emotions—even physical reactions can result."[11] In *Virtual Reality: Through the New Looking Glass*, Ken Pimentel and Kevin Teixeira explain that VR requires "the same mental shift that happens when you get wrapped up in a good novel or become absorbed in playing a computer game."[12] Joining in on the wave of excitement about the digital, literary scholars seized this comparison as well. Perhaps the most prominent is Janet Murray's *Hamlet on the Holodeck: The Future of Narrative in Cyberspace*, which imagines literature composed in a medium like *Star Trek: The Next Generation*'s perfected simulation facility.[13] "The age-old desire to live out a fantasy aroused by a fictional world," Murray writes, "has been intensified by a participatory, immersive medium that promises to satisfy it more completely than has ever before been possible."[14]

Submerged in the Virtual

This continuity between print and digital media rests on their presumed immersive capacity.[15] Placing it first in her list of literary qualities of the VR medium, Murray defines immersion as a border-crossing experience: "Immersion is a metaphorical term derived from the physical experience of being submerged in water. We seek the same feeling from a psychologically immersive experience that we do from a plunge in the ocean or swimming pool: the sensation of being surrounded by a completely other reality, as different as water is from air, that takes over all of our attention, our whole perceptual apparatus."[16] The subject looking into a computer monitor in the real world gives her full attention to the virtual world appearing on-screen, resulting in this experience of slipping beneath the surface. She submits her "whole perceptual apparatus" to the virtual while not acknowledging the device that projects it. This model of immersion, on which the connection between digital and print media depends, thus produces an ontological binary, a physical reality in opposition to "a completely other" virtual reality. As Pimentel and Teixeira explain by way of Coleridge, "the question isn't whether the created world is as real as the physical world, but whether the created world is real enough for you to suspend your disbelief for a period of time."[17]

Under the immersion model of first-generation VR research—and, by extension, the literary theory it inspires—a fictional, "virtual" reality overcomes the subject's awareness of what Theodor Nelson calls the "irrelevant 'reality' of implementation details."[18] Castronova writes that VR research began with the belief that computers could generate sensations so convincing that they would seem real, "but because those sensations would be computer generated, they would be not 'really real' but only 'virtually real.'"[19] Resonating with Murray's definition, Frank Biocca and Ben Delaney explain that immersivity is "the degree to which a virtual environment submerges the perceptual system of the user in computer-generated stimuli. The more the system blocks out stimuli from the physical world, the more the system is considered to be immersive."[20]

The Matrix offers an image of a perfected version of this understanding of immersion, an understanding that had spread from science labs to the popular imaginary. In order to jack in to the computer simulation known as the Matrix while on Morpheus's hovercraft in the real world, Neo inserts a needled cable into a port at the base of his head. This connection subverts awareness of the plugged-in body, supplanting it with a sense of presence in a computer simulation. Jacking-in redirects Neo's consciousness, taking him out of the physical experience of his body, which, when aboard the hovercraft, is strapped into a chair, and reorients him within the computer-generated environment, where he can dodge bullets, fly, and so on. The VR experience is brought about by manipulating input to the spinal column in

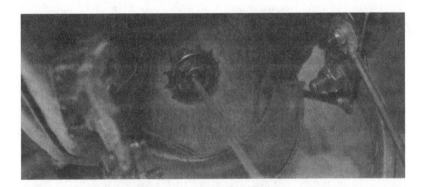

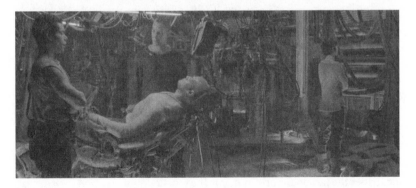

FIGURE 1.1. The port at the base of Neo's skull accepts the sensor input that will immerse him in computer simulations like the Matrix. The second view shows the hovercraft's immersion apparatus. Morpheus, with his embodied perception of the ship's hull replaced by the Matrix, lies prone while jacked in. From *The Matrix*.

such a convincing way that the immediate sensation of the metal chair, the discomfort of the input needle, spatial awareness of the ship's hull, and so forth, are trumped by sensory input piped into the brain.[21]

Immersion, under this model, is understood as a problem of user interface. As Marie-Laure Ryan notes, "'Virtual reality' is not just the ultimate medium, it is the ultimate interface metaphor."[22] For it to work, the computer has to stimulate the senses without being detected as the source of the stimulation. "Computers are liminal objects," Murray writes, "located on the threshold between external reality and our own minds," and maintaining this threshold is essential to the immersive experience.[23] In order to achieve the "induced illusion [that] was the stated purpose of early VR research," a great deal of resources went into "refining sensory-delivery devices" and "reducing the clumsiness of the apparatus."[24] This interface research resulted in many of the technologies now typically associated with a "standardized vision of VR."[25] If the subject is conscious of the apparatus, then she cannot be "within" a projected world because at some level she is aware that in reality it is only a projection. Therefore, transparency of the medium is "a precondition for total immersion in a medium-created world."[26]

The Problem with Literature

This kind of medium transparency presents a challenge for immersion in print literature. Ryan takes the VR-literature comparison to its furthest extent, attempting to derive "a general theory of representation and communication"[27] from Pimentel and Teixeira's definition of VR as "an immersive, interactive experience generated by a computer."[28] Even so, she recognized that this immersive capacity is always limited in comparison to VR because print literature has only language to "substitute for all channels of sensation."[29] A VR system can involve all manner of sensory input device— headsets, headphones, gloves, even whole rooms—in order to "[block] out stimuli from the physical world."[30] Literature, on the other hand, merely describes the fictional world and only the most relevant portions of it at that. It thus leaves a great deal for the reader to fill in with imagination and personal experience; books must rely on "the reader's proficiency in performing the necessary world-building operations."[31]

Furthermore, this "active process of construction" must go unnoticed by the reader. Just as with VR, when the subject—in this case a reader—is aware of the "irrelevant 'reality' of implantations details," she is aware that the fictional world is constructed and therefore not real.[32] Luckily, readers have become very good at this "fictional game" and "take it for granted that worlds should emerge from texts."[33] Still, "language has to make itself invisible in order to create immersion" even as the reader engages with it to co-construct a virtual reality.[34]

Immersion, under a first-generation VR model, is threatened by the interactivity of print literature because it disrupts fictional recentering.[35] According to Ryan, the immersed reader suspends disbelief to accept the axes of what is actual and what is possible in the world of the text and is "transported" there. To acknowledge the active process of construction, then, is to recognize that the text describes a possible world, a virtual reality, rather than the actual one, and reorient oneself within one's "native" world.[36] Therefore immersion is a function of this capacity to generate and maintain a convincingly realistic, self-contained fictional universe—or, in short, realism.

The Immersive Promise of True Fiction

Ryan's "poetics of immersion" take the form of an "illusionist conception," which recalls the "induced illusion" of VR.[37] A text achieves this mode of realism "when it creates a credible, seemingly autonomous and language-independent reality, when the style of depiction captures an aura of presence, when the reader is imaginatively part of the textual world and senses that there is more to this world than what the text displays of it."[38] The nineteenth-century novel "perfected" this mode, which is less about representing reality than it is about "getting the reader involved in narrated events." Despite relying on "the least natural, most ostentatiously fictional of narrative techniques," literary realism can remain relatively transparent as it is meant to pass for the "spontaneous inscription of events."[39] It thus constitutes the literary equivalent of the "natural language" to which VR aspires.[40] Further, though the events described in a realist novel did not actually happen, they are conceived of as at least possible given historical circumstances. Even if *Madame Bovary* isn't "true" in a traditional sense, it is set in the "real" world, which makes it relatively easy for readers to access its fictional universe.

Following this logic a little further, a genre of fiction even more immersively accessible than the nineteen-century novel would apply a realist literary style to narrativize actual events. In other words, it would be a nonfiction novel, like *In Cold Blood*. Ryan ranks *In Cold Blood* as the "best known example" of "true fiction," or fact-based narratives that make no claim to truth.[41] Because Truman Capote's 1966 novel is based on facts, it is "epistemically accessible from the real world, in so far as everything we know about reality can be integrated into it." However, because it isn't necessarily objective or true, *In Cold Blood* remains one possible account of how actual events might have occurred. As a true fiction, *In Cold Blood* presents itself as an image of the actual world, though it remains merely possible, still fictional, and thus still available to immersed recentering.[42]

New Journalism: Beyond the Binary

In theory, *In Cold Blood* represents an ideal of immersive literature approaching the example set by first-generation VR systems. Yet this immersive model depends on an ontological binary, which the nonfiction novel problematizes as a central component of its aesthetic. As Tom Wolfe explains, a New Journalist project depends on and proceeds from "the simple fact that the reader knows *all this actually happened*."[43] It expects that readers recognize the circumstances of production—in other words, they recognize the story they read is a narrative account based on the author's extensive factual research. Their awareness generates a paradoxical sense of eerie proximity to actual historical events and, in the case of *In Cold Blood*, real deaths, enabled and endangered by the author's acknowledged mediating influence. In other words, the New Journalism aesthetic relies on the reader's understanding that it is an account of true events, a particularly informed interpretation that, nonetheless, invites, often to the consternation of the author, skepticism.

Though problematic for immersive reading, true fiction's capacity to productively hold in abeyance the tension between the fictional and the actual exemplifies an integrated engagement of media-generated virtuality and material contexts. Many have read Wolfe's oft-quoted declaration, "*all this actually happened*," as a truth claim. Taken in context, however, Wolfe makes no claim for the New Journalism work detailing what *"actually happened"* in reality. Instead, he makes a straightforward, uncontroversial statement about fiction based on real events as compared to fiction based on imaginative invention. Wolfe's point is that New Journalism benefits from the unique way it positions the audience in relation to the story told: "For the gluttonous Goths there is still only the outlaw's rule regarding technique: take, use, improvise. The result is a form that is not merely *like a novel*. It consumes devices that happen to have originated with the novel and mixes them with every other device known to prose. And all the while, quite beyond matters of technique, it enjoys an advantage so obvious, so built-in, one almost forgets what a power it has: the simple fact that the reader knows *all this actually happened*." Wolfe emphasizes the literary qualities of New Journalism in this passage. New Journalism is not reporting that reads like a novel, or "a contemporary genre in which journalistic material is presented in the forms of fiction."[44] Instead, Wolfe describes it as a new literary genre that "consumes devices" from all manner of prose, journalism and fiction included.

Furthermore, Wolfe does not claim that this all-consuming style is more realistic. Rather, it is more "powerful" because the piece is based on a true story: "The disclaimers have been erased. The screen is gone. The writer is one step closer to the absolute involvement of the reader that Henry James and James Joyce dreamed of and never achieved."[45] Because the work of New Journalism describes a historical event, it does the heroes of high modernism one better. Whereas Henry James attempted an almost voyeuristic vantage on a fictional world and Joyce developed stream of consciousness to put readers into his characters' heads, a New Journalist begins with the reader already situated within the reality of the story's happening.

The "screen" that in fiction protects the reader with the knowledge that what she reads is not "real" has been removed, leaving open the possibility that she could somehow be involved. There is no need to disclaim any coincidental correspondence to real events because the reader is always already *in* the world of the story. They are always already immersed and, furthermore, they know it.

Wolfe makes two assumptions about what the reader knows when describing the aesthetic power of fact-based novels. First, the reader is aware that the events described correspond to historical events, even if described inaccurately. Second, the reader is also aware that the text they are holding is based on those events. The "*all this*" in Wolfe's statement does double duty, referring to both the events described and the compilation of research forming that description. In other words, removing the screen reveals the projector.

If this fiction-screen is understood as a disclaimer granting the reader permission to disengage what happens in the story from the real world, it would also have the effect of obscuring the implementation details, which in the case of the nonfiction novel would include the material book, the backstory of the author's research, the physical task of reading, and so on. Once that screen is gone, the reader is one step closer to being involved in the narrative but is already absolutely involved in the telling of that narrative. Fundamental to the aesthetic experience of New Journalism, and thus its ability to produce affective immersion, is the reader's consciousness, at some level, of a world and history external to the text and the place of the text they are holding within that world.[46] Therefore, engagement depends on the reader's encounter with the text transpiring in the actual world and, thus, on her *not* being fully recentered. Its reality effect is a function of the reader's situatedness in the real world.

Embodied Readership

In this respect, the New Journalism aesthetic relies on what N. Katherine Hayles calls its embodiment. Embodiment for Hayles is not synonymous with "the body"; rather, it is an "articulation" of material contexts: "In contrast to the body, embodiment is contextual, enmeshed with the specifics of place, time, physiology, and culture, which together compose enactment."[47] With a view to embodiment, the simple statement "it is raining"—to use one of Hayles's examples—extends beyond the immediate position of the speaking body relative to the falling water, the chemical composition and characteristics of that water, and the feeling of being caught in the rain to include also the local, historical, and cultural significance of rain and being wet.[48] In Seattle, for example, "it is raining" is conditioned by the fact that most Seattleites are so accustomed to the climate that they do not feel the need to carry umbrellas. If we add to this local attitude socioeconomic factors—whether or not the interlocutors work outside, their proximity to

Seattle's homeless population, public funding for shelter and transportation that would get people out of the rain, and so on—we begin to see the network of contextual factors put into play by embodiment.

With regard to literature, this understanding of embodiment has allowed Hayles to demonstrate how a user's interactions with an inscription technology—be it print or digital—shape the imaginative world it generates.[49] However, as is apparent from Wolfe's description, New Journalism reveals how embodied readership extends out into the world away from the text. Indeed, the events described in a work of New Journalism are articulated with their "actual happening," which are themselves "enmeshed" in a host of historical, material, and social contexts as well. If, as Wolfe suggests, the screen truly is gone in New Journalism, then its embodied readers belong to a feedback circuit joining the fictional to the material to the cultural.

Not coincidentally, tracing these circuits became particularly important during the 1990s. Writing at the height of the dot-com hype, Hayles observes that the advances in cybernetics, informatics, and digital applications—including first-generation VR—rely on a theory of information decoupled from material instantiation. As digital communication technologies spread, "help[ing] to make an information theoretic view a part of everyday life," the perception that information "interpenetrates" and is "more mobile, more important, and more *essential* than material forms" entered the cultural mindset.[50] Under this "condition of virtuality," information is understood as "free-floating, unaffected by changes in context," and is thus abstracted from the network of co-responsive material factors that give it meaning. Hayles's affirmation of the role of embodiment in communication attempts to recuperate the significance of contextual particularities.

To that end, the model of situated reading that Wolfe describes seems perfectly suited to integrating the virtualities of fiction with the material conditions of their enactment. Wolfe suggests that such an aesthetic experience is specific to New Journalism, owing to the fact that it describes events that "*actually happened.*" Hayles argues, however, that embodiment is an irreducible property of all communication. It may be possible, therefore, to read a nonfiction novel, like *In Cold Blood*, not as merely the best-known example of an idiosyncratic genre, but as a model of readership, as making explicit a more general property of the literary.

2 Reading *In Cold Blood* Today

Toward a Model of Mixed Realism

As digital communication technologies entered the home in the 1990s, they were joined to the history and future of print fiction through their shared capacity for immersion. The model of immersion used in these comparisons demands a clear distinction between a generated virtual reality and the "real" reality of the physical world. The immersiveness of markedly distinct media—both print and digital—was thereby understood as a function of their ability to avoid signaling ontological discrepancies between the projected worlds and the real one. Under this model, Truman Capote's *In Cold Blood*, Marie-Laure Ryan's prototypical "true fiction," is exemplary of immersive literature.[1] "Deliberately conceived and presented as an accurate image of reality," Capote's novel hides ontological discrepancies particularly well and, thus, could more easily draw readers into a "fictional universe."

In Cold Blood, however, cannot affirm the required differentiation of the factual and the fictional on which this model of immersion depends. Rather, at the heart of Capote's nonfiction novel is a paradox that a binary model cannot resolve, one that folds back on the task of reading itself. This chapter returns to this pivotal text in the history of immersive media in order to demonstrate how the ambivalence of Capote's "factual" account might offer an integrated model of readership more suited to a mixed reality paradigm.

The Paradox of the Nonfiction Novel

During his well-known 1966 interview following the release of *In Cold Blood*, George Plimpton asks Truman Capote about "the temptation to fictionalize events" when writing a nonfiction novel.[2] He notes specifically the convenient appearance of dogs at the end of one section and at the beginning of another, and suggests that Capote might have invented them "as a fiction device to bridge the two sections." Capote responded with characteristic snark: "No. There was a dog, and it was precisely as described. One doesn't spend almost six years on a book, the point of which is factual accuracy, and then give way to minor distortions. People are so suspicious."

Indeed people had been suspicious of Capote's claims to nonfiction from the moment of its serialized publication in the *New Yorker* 1965, and not entirely without justification.[3] Knowing, as he did, that his journalistic integrity was in question, the logic of Capote's defense in the Plimpton interview is unexpected. Expanding on his initial response, Capote explains how he managed to "reconstruct the conversation of a dead girl, Nancy Clutter, without fictionalizing":

> If they read the book carefully, they can see readily enough how it's done. It's a silly question. Each time Nancy appears in the narrative, there are witnesses to what she is saying and doing—phone calls, conversations, being overheard. When she walks the horse up from the river in the twilight, the hired man is a witness and talked to her then. The last time we see her, in her bedroom, Perry and Dick themselves were the witnesses, and told me what she had said. What is reported of her, even in the narrative form, is as accurate as many hours of questioning, over and over again, can make it. All of it is reconstructed from the evidence of witnesses which is implicit in the title of the first section of the book "The Last to See Them Alive."[4]

Because Capote only had witness accounts and secondhand quotations to go on, the murdered Nancy Clutter could only appear in the story within earshot of another person. Rather than responding with a defense of his objectivity, an explanation of his research methods, or an appeal to his sources, Capote cites the constraints that testimonial evidence put on the construction of the narrative.

Accused of invention, Capote asserts that "narrative form" attests to his factual accuracy, that reality is confirmed in his artifice. But it was precisely the constructedness, the "narrative form," that raised suspicions about his nonfiction novel in the first place. In the introduction to his anthology of New Journalism, Tom Wolfe notes that the "esthetic dimension" of the nonfiction novel often inspires readers to suspect *"the bastards are making it up!"*[5] For this reason, the negotiation between authorial control and factual presentation is the "crucial problem for a new journalist."[6] Yet it is a problem that—importantly—is never fully resolved.

As discussed in the previous chapter, the defining characteristic of the New Journalism—"the simple fact that the reader knows *all this actually happened"*—applies equally to the story told and the process of its telling.[7] Readers are aware that these narratives describe historical events and that an author who investigated those events now mediates their access to them. The artfulness with which Capote uses testimonial evidence—as when he "[reconstructs] the conversations of a dead girl"—belies facticity because it implies fabrication. The reader's suspicions, therefore, likely could not be settled by more attentive reading, as Capote suggests. Nor will fact-checking Capote's research subvert the accomplishment of his nonfiction novel. Rather, both arise from the fundamental ambivalence between the true and the invented, which Capote's project animates.

In Cold Blood explores the role of narrativization in American culture as it shapes Capote's own telling of the Clutter family's murder and the ensuing investigation, trial, and execution. From the rumor that brought the murderers Dick Hickock and Perry Smith to the Clutter family farm to the conflicting confessions that led to their execution and all the speculations in between, *In Cold Blood* shows the factual and the fictional as they interact and overlap in "real life" and with deadly consequences. Multiple nonfiction narratives—witness statements, town gossip, police reports, suspect confessions—at varying levels of authority and objectivity commingle in Capote's own. Further, the reader's own attempt to reconstruct "all that actually happened" from the layers of mediation and interpretation is folded into the complex co-articulations of events and their retellings. Thus, no matter how "factually accurate" it is, *In Cold Blood* inevitably fails to offer the definitive, objective report on what happened in Holcomb, Kansas, on November 14,

1959, the night the Clutters died. Instead, its failure demonstrates—and each reading enacts anew—the entanglement of the factual and the fictional.

Capote's Paradoxical Presence

Some critics have gotten tied up attempting to straighten *In Cold Blood* out, calling for the nonfiction novel to declare itself on one side of an ontological binary. Phyllis Frus, for example, criticizes Capote's choice not to make his presence known throughout *In Cold Blood*: "If we have no mention of an author or an equivalent source of the plot, we are liable to presume an omniscient author of an invented tale, or the absolute world of distant history."[8] On these grounds, Frus prefers Norman Mailer's nonfiction novel *The Executioner's Song*, published by Little, Brown in 1979, for detailing the process of securing the rights to convicted murderer Garry Gilmore's story. Capote, on the other hand, leaves himself out of *In Cold Blood* and avoids all mention of his research or interaction with the people in his story. As a result, Frus argues, his fact-based account reads as if it were invented. The implication, then, is that if he had noted his participation in the scenes he described, his account would come off as more factual. Doing so, however, implies a contradiction.

The appearance of the author's hand is still customarily taken as evidence of a text's construction, its fabrication, its artfulness, and thus its deceitfulness, despite the fact that such an appearance lays bare the reality of the text as such. Awareness of the author reminds us that a text was, in reality, authored. Reporting on its own "process of production," as Frus requests, has the paradoxical effect of making a work more real by making it more artificial.

According to Ryan's immersive model, this kind of self-reference points back to the actual world and makes the reader conscious of her "actively mediating presence," the "price" of which is "loss of membership in the fictional world."[9] The only way a novel can become "real" to its readers is by covering up its process of production through artful construction. It is moments like the one Capote explains to Plimpton, in which the "process of production" is so artfully obscured as to go unnoticed, when *In Cold Blood* is most realistic. Yet, perhaps the fact that Capote has to answer inquiries regarding Nancy's scenes suggests that he has not sufficiently covered his tracks—that his fact-based reconstruction is not artificial enough.

Evidence and Artifice

This paradox is exemplified throughout the novel in Capote's use of quotation, which testifies simultaneously to the story's factual basis and its constructedness. For example, we are told about the night prior to the murder, Saturday, through an extended quotation from Bobby Rupp in which he "described his last visit to the Clutter home."[10] The quotation, however, comes from his testimony prior to a lie-detector test that took place on "the following Monday." At this point in the narrative, it is only Saturday, November 14, the murders haven't been committed yet, and Bobby won't become a suspect for another twenty-plus pages. Even so, the appearance of Rupp's statement means the reader has been situated sometime after Monday, November 16, after the murders, able to hear the testimony of suspects.

Of course, this would have been Capote's position as well. He obviously did not arrive in Holcomb until after the murders, so his access to those events came via interviews and testimonials. The story Rupp tells during his lie-detector session was likely Capote's own source for that night's events, just as it is for his readers. Rather than inventing his own summary account, he seems to simply insert Rupp's testimony, whole cloth. The night before the Clutter murders is, thus, literally and narratively reconstructed from witness accounts.

More often than not Capote is willing to let the characters speak for themselves, but he clearly wants his readers to know it. The scene in which Nancy Ewalt and Susan Kidwell find the slain family is narrated by Susan, "in a statement made at a later date," apparently inserted directly (59). Readers gain access to the crime scene and have their first encounter with the mutilated bodies via Larry Hendricks's first-person account as "said to an acquaintance," whom we can only assume was Capote, which is quoted extensively (61). Capote repeatedly uses witness testimonies in this way to deliver the narrative. The effect of this method is twofold. Inserting apparently unaltered statements conveys transparency and objectivity: the story straight from those who were there, with no intervention from the author. Capote would seem to put to his readers the same evidence with which he has pieced together his account. Paradoxically, however, his attempt to give us his same direct access also distances the reader from the events, situating us apart and after. We, quite literally, learn of this story thirdhand, from Hendricks to

Capote to us. So, while this narration through quotation attests to the text's objectivity as based on direct testimony from those who were there and implies the actual putting together of the narrative, it simultaneously emphasizes the constructedness of the text, the layers of mediation that constitute evidence and access, and the insurmountable distance between the reader and all that "*actually happened.*"

Occasionally, selected phrases in a paragraph of exposition will appear in quotations for no apparent reason other than to suggest fidelity to a source. For example, in a paragraph explaining why Nancy Ewalt visited the Clutters on Sunday morning, it is unclear why Capote quotes "making two back-and-forth trips to town," "barging right in," and "utility room," other than to prove he is working from firsthand accounts (58). Likewise, quotations frequently justify Capote's paraphrasing. In the following passage in which he wants to demonstrate the basis for claiming to know Dick's thoughts, Capote places a validating statement in parenthesis after the narration in question: "Yesterday, after studying the papers, Perry had put the same question, and Dick, who thought he'd disposed of it ('Look, if those cowboys could make the slightest connection, we'd have heard the sound of hoofs a hundred miles off'), was bored at hearing it again" (90). These authentications often appear at the expense of believability. For example, before returning from Mexico, Perry sat outside the hotel trying to decide what of his belongings he could carry with him. As he "look[s] through old letters, photographs, clippings, and selected mementos," Perry drifts into a long reflection on his life story starting at age three and proceeding chronologically up to a letter he received from his sister in 1958 (125). This reflection is carried out through several inset stories, reenactments of past conversations, clips from actual letters, and so on, and flits in and out of tenses depending on source material. Despite being "objectively" gathered and pasted directly into the story, Perry's reflections undermine the credibility of the underlying narrative. It seems all too convenient a way to flesh out Perry's past without diverging too much from the cramped timeline at hand. It's a clichéd flashback moment. Even if we were to accept that something like this rather-thorough reminiscing actually happened, its execution does not attempt to hide its construction. Passages of third-person past-tense narration are interrupted by extended quotations, clumsily introduced, with "as Perry recalled" (132).

Capote definitely could have woven these moments into the chronology of the narrative by excluding the qualifiers in much the same way he couched the clippings of old letters into this story about going through old mementos. Instead, Capote refuses to obscure the fact that this is a reconstruction based on evidence after the fact. As a result, these moments appear as reflections on reflecting: "As Perry recalled, 'I was always thinking about Dad, hoping he could come take me away, and I remember, like a second ago, the time I saw him again.'" In fact, some of these quotations are introduced with "Perry once said," suggesting explicitly that the reflection to follow took place on another occasion (133). Perry is quoted from a different time-space than that of the immediate narrative moment. In order to preserve the objectivity of the narrative he is presenting, Capote has superimposed onto the narrative chronology of the Clutter family's murder and Dick and Perry's trial a second chronology corresponding to Capote's own piecing together of his account, as if to give license to his dramatization.

In this way, Capote attempts to provide justification for his narrative by granting direct access to his research materials. Doing so, however, emphasizes his presence in the text by exposing the layers of mediation between the historical events and us as readers. In effect, Capote's effort to keep us close to the source material constructs the implied, parallel narrative of his own project, of his own construction of what happened. Frus, therefore, may get what she wants—disclosure of the tale's origins—but we are no closer to being able to separate fact from fiction. If not from its detail and style, from whence does *In Cold Blood* receive its reality effect?

Involving the Reader

Rather than pursuing this insight into New Journalism, I want to consider the implications for discussions of immersive media in the digital age. As discussed in the previous chapter, *In Cold Blood* played a minor though not insignificant role in literary scholars' endorsement of the dot-com hype of the early 1990s, serving as a model of literary immersion comparable to that of first-generation VR systems. The model of immersion that formed the basis of that comparison, however, depends on an ontological binary that neither print nor digital media can sustain, a fact exemplified by Capote's novel itself. As shown above, Capote's inclusion of facts in the form of

quotations from testimony reveals a deep-seated ambivalence in his reconstruction that cannot be resolved into either objective fact or invented fiction.
Rather than immerse its readers, the novel confronts them with the ambivalence of "factual" accounts even as they know all along that "*all this actually
happened.*"

In the previous chapter, I also compared Tom Wolfe's description of New
Journalism's aesthetic principles favorably with N. Katherine Hayles's concept of embodiment, which she presents as an alternative to immersion models. As a work of New Journalism, *In Cold Blood* clearly benefits from this
kind of embodied readership. The novel's entire conceit and success depends
on the reader knowing that the Clutters were actually murdered and that
Dick and Perry were actually hanged. However, beyond knowing that the
novel depicts a historical event, it also testifies to the historical event of its
own composition. It uses this recognition to both themeatize narrative making as a core issue in the trial as well as enact an ambivalent relationship
between the factual and the fictional relevant to the trial and to the task of
reading about it. In doing so, *In Cold Blood* subverts its immersive potential
by integrating the reader's task of reading the novel with the core problematic of fact-based narrativization.

While some like Ryan, who want to commit the novel to fiction, or Frus,
who want to commit it to fact, will try to unify *In Cold Blood* by collapsing
this paradox to one side of the binary, to do so misses the point. With enough
research, one can identify and correct Capote's factual errors; in fact, not
a few people have endeavored to do just that.[11] New Journalism, however,
never intended to present the definitive factual account of historical events.
Rather, New Journalism is an aesthetic project concerned with the effects
of factually based fictions. In other words, it is interested in what happens
when we cannot address a story through a clear distinction between realms.

The New Journalist novel specifically calls on readers to give up on sepa-
rating fact from fiction and instead to focus on how the two are folded
together. Such is the call made by *In Cold Blood* as Capote's quotation of
witness statements overlays his task of composing the story on to the narrated events. Taken on its own, the resulting narrative of multiple homicide,
trial, and execution is severely disjointed, lacking a basic consistency of time
and place as the novel constantly shifts its locus between the fictionalized

account of what happened and the location of hindsight from which the account was compiled. In this disjointedness, however, *In Cold Blood* lays bare to some degree its "process of production."

Capote's inclusion of apparently unaltered testimony puts the reader before the very evidence on which his account is based. These direct quotations simultaneously attest to the facticity, transparency, and veracity of Capote's narrative and reveal that our only access to these or any historical events are second- or, in this case, thirdhand. The actual events of 1959 remain impenetrable, set back into the past by their telling and the layers of mediation written into the text itself. But what more could we ask of Capote's version besides access to the evidence on which he built his case? Those witness accounts, those facts on which the case against Perry and Dick was prosecuted, on which Capote grounded his narrative, still mediate access to the actual events to this day. If our interest is in knowing what happened in 1959, our only way of finding out is through textual research, which will turn up more accounts like Capote's, narrativizations based on the stories told by the people who were there. In a sense, we as readers, with the same evidence he used, are tasked with the same project as Capote himself: piece a bunch of witness testimonies into the story of what happened. Capote's quotations therefore both support his version and introduce the possibility that the reader could construct the story differently.

Yes, our access to the events of the story are filtered through Capote, and so the story we get is arranged according to what he thought was important; yes, we have to trust that he actually did remember the content of his interviews verbatim; and, yes, it is possible he would sacrifice some factual details for his art. But, at the same time, at no point does Capote's account completely settle the story it is telling. *In Cold Blood* is not a proper mystery because we know the who, what, where, and when from the get-go; all that is left is the why and how. That is to say, we know the facts, but not the narrative.

Overlapping Narrativizations

The project of the book is the (re)construction of this story, and it cannot remind us often enough. Of course, *In Cold Blood* represents Capote's substantial effort to write the narrative of what happened in Holcomb; and, as Wolfe's descriptions of New Journalism make clear, it is necessary that the reader recognize the novel's project. But in addition to Capote's story writing, the novel itself is rife with similar attempts to come up with the story of what went down the night of the murders. This multiplication of the narrative, in turn, invites the reader construct an account herself.

Throughout, but especially before Dick and Perry are arrested, we are introduced to townspeople like Postmistress Clare, who offer their own guesses as to who-done-it and why. "What a terrible thing," Clare comments, "when neighbors can't look at each other without kind of wondering!" (70). The townspeople's speculation is formalized by the ongoing criminal investigation, which is itself the official, public, legal account of what happened. Chapters focusing on the investigators' "pursuit of the narrative" function like plot summaries, reviewing the evidence available at the time and presenting working theories, interpretations, and dramatizations of the facts at hand (222). Again, Capote lets the character, in this example Kansas Bureau of Investigation agent Harold Nye, speak for himself: "But none of the persons he questioned, and none of the questions he asked ('I was exploring the emotional background. I thought the answer might be another woman—a triangle. Well, consider: Mr. Clutter was a fairly young, very healthy man, but his wife, she was a semi-invalid, she slept in a separate bedroom ...'), produced useful information" (85). The investigators were also frequently working from stories, first-person testimonies like that of Bobby Rupp. In fact, the tip that broke the case—Floyd Wells recalling that while in prison Dick had told him about his plot to rob the Clutters—is called a story, "tale-telling" that "might easily" have been "invented" (189). The criminal investigation thus stages and parallels Capote's own task of constructing the narrative of all that "*actually happened*" from facts and testimony. Furthermore, just like Capote's version, even though their story is based on sound evidence the investigators are unable to demarcate a clear line between fact and fiction.

Even when the investigators have enough evidence to prosecute, their final account of all that happened remains unconfirmed. The climactic scene in which Perry finally gives his point-by-point recounting of the murders ends up introducing its own uncertainties. At this point, Dick had already confessed so investigators could ask detailed questions aimed at nailing down the exact sequence of events ("Duntz says, 'Perry, I've been keeping track of the lights. The way I calculate it, when you turned off the upstairs lights, that left the house completely dark'") and compare versions in order to confirm the story ("[KBI investigator Alvin] Dewey admits it, but he adds that except for an apparently somewhat expurgated version of his own conduct, Hickock's story supports Smith's. The details vary, the dialogue is not identical, but in substance the two accounts—thus far, at least—corroborate one another") (243). The two confessions confirmed that the tandem had committed the murders. Who had done what, however, remained unsettled: "the only serious discrepancy being that Hickock attributed all four deaths to Smith, while Smith contended that Hickock had killed the two women" (245). Even with two confessions it was still unclear whether Dick had killed anyone.

A month later, Perry refuses to sign his statement and asks to change his confession to "admit that Hickock had been telling the truth, and that it was he, Perry Smith, who had shot and killed the whole family" (255). Perry tells Dewey that he had originally lied to "fix Dick for being such a coward" but

FIGURE 2.1. Forty years after the events covered in Truman Capote's *In Cold Blood*, the residents of the former Clutter home play in the basement where Herb Clutter and his son Kenyon were found dead. Photograph by Kris Kolden.

now wants to set the record straight out of consideration for Dick's "real sweet" mother: "It might be some comfort to her to know Dick never pulled the trigger." Though this new version clears up the sole remaining discrepancy in the two accounts, Dewey states, "I wasn't certain I believed it. Not to the extent of letting him alter his statement." He goes on to explain that the actual details, the true account of "exactly what happened in that house that night" is unnecessary to move forward with their murder case: "With or without it, we had enough to hang them ten times over" (256). Dewey proves to be correct. Dick and Perry are hanged, and the novel ends without ever giving the reader a definitive, factual, or even reliable account of what happened the night of the murders. Furthermore, if Perry was honestly setting the story straight, then the legal record of those events, which was the grounds on which two men were executed, is fictional.

In Cold Blood folds on top of one another three attempts to construct the story of what happened to the Clutter family. First, there are the attempts by the townspeople and investigators, who gathered the evidence, interviewed witnesses and suspects, and presented them as a case against Perry and Dick. Second, there is Capote's research, conducted largely alongside the official investigation, and subsequent compilation into the nonfiction narrative *In Cold Blood*. Finally, there is the present-time reader of *In Cold Blood*, who via Capote's inclusion of unedited quotations, pieces together her own understanding of what happened. While this final setting—that of the reader—is centrally influenced by Capote's arrangement, Capote certainly is not the only source of information about the Clutter family's murder. *In Cold Blood*, the novel, has always existed in a larger media ecology, beginning with the sparse newspaper article that inspired the project. Now, in the age of the online database, a simple Google search returns a preponderance of information, images—like the ones included here—and video clips, all easily accessible for readers of *In Cold Blood* seeking to supplement Capote's account.

Individual readers may or may not pursue these other sources, but that is not the point. Capote's fictionalized version does not exist in a vacuum; it is imbricated with multiple other attempts to narrativize those events, including that of the present-day reader. These overlapping interpretations produce a feedback loop informing and reconstituting one another, extending the events of 1959, and Capote's project, in perpetuity. The screen Wolfe talks about is undeniably gone. The question to ask, then, is not where is the line between fact and fiction, between true account and fictionalization, but, rather, what is the significance and the consequence of these co-articulated narrativizations and the exchanges between them?

Readers of *In Cold Blood* have access to the world of the novel at a level unimaginable to binary immersion models like the one Ryan shares with first-generation VR. Of course there is the nonfiction aspect, which means the events described correspond to an actual historical event, but it goes beyond that. The reader of *In Cold Blood* is confronted with the core problematic animating the narrative, that access to all that "actually happened" is always mediated and thus always contains an element of storytelling, of the virtual, of the fictional.

Capote's nonfiction novel is therefore both a story of and a performance of the entanglement of fact and fiction. Each time it is read, it enacts the inadequacy of that binary despite the sometimes life-and-death consequences of its application. So when I take up *In Cold Blood* and find the traces of

FIGURE 2.2. The former bedroom of Bonnie Clutter, where her body was found forty years earlier. Photograph by Kris Kolden.

Capote's hand—the awkwardly integrated quotations, inconsistencies in tense, and so on—alongside gaps in the prosecution's narrative, I, too, must contend with all that stands between me and the events themselves; I, too, perform a paradoxical articulation of fact and fiction. The screen is indeed gone, but in more ways than Wolfe probably imagined. Without a disclaimer and its reassurance that the events described will stay on their side of the screen, I confront the events themselves as a part of my historical reality as well as the unsettling possibility that I might be "absolutely involved" in their real-world implications and consequences.

The ambiguous relationship between fact and fiction is the core problematic engaged by the characters, Capote, and the reader, all of whom try to reconstruct the narrative of the murders. In this way, *In Cold Blood* establishes a circuit of interaction that connects the investigation to Capote's research to the present-day reader. This circuit, however, extends beyond the reader's interaction with the text. Capote's novel also ends up being about the way entanglements of fact and fiction participate in the social fabric of small towns (Holcomb), about interpersonal relationships (between Dick and Perry, in

FIGURE 2.3. Finney County Courthouse in Garden City, Kansas, where Dick and Perry stood trial, as it looked in 2005. Photograph by Kris Kolden.

particular), and about the legal system in the United States (in the investigation and trial). Capote, then, has removed the screen by revealing screens everywhere in U.S. social life.

More than simply representing these real-world dynamics, Capote's discussion of these settings establishes them as the context for the reader's own encounter with and performance of the fact/fiction binary that the novel initiates. For example, rather than just telling a story that highlights the factual ambiguities in Dick and Perry's case, *In Cold Blood* requires that readers deal with and construct a narrative around those ambiguities, just as Dewey and the investigators had to, as a function of reading the novel. In this way, the act of reading becomes a performance of the very problematic Capote's novel suggests is inherent in U.S. legal system.[12] With the screen gone the reader is susceptible to the absolute involvement, and thus Capote's narrativized account is able to implicate her act of reading in real-world contexts and consequences.

While it is of course possible to map the various circuits uniting narrative to reading to real-world context that *In Cold Blood* facilitates, doing so is beyond the scope of this chapter. My goal, rather, has been to demonstrate an approach to narrative fiction that sidesteps ontological binaries in order to address the virtualities of fiction as integrated with the practices of everyday life—that is, a mixed realism.

The compatibility of first-generation VR theory and Ryan's narratology is the result of an assumed binary opposition between media-generated virtualities and the material world. Not only has this immersion model of user–machine interface been superseded by a mixed reality paradigm that more accurately describes our everyday encounters with the virtual, but it is also a symptom of the "condition of virtuality."[13] Hayles's own redefinition of embodiment offers a way to think about a user's interaction with the virtual as an articulation of "place, time, physiology, and culture," rather than some kind of border crossing.[14]

Capote's *In Cold Blood* exemplifies this model, incorporating the very task of reading it into its layers of interdependent narrativizations. Attempting to piece together what happened in Holcomb, the reader must contend with the ambivalence of fact and fiction, not within a possible world but within the same historical reality in which the Clutters died. *In Cold Blood* thus goes beyond a representation of the role of the factual and the fictional in the practice of everyday life to *enact* that role through the real-world practice of reading it. In other words, the novel is integrated with the embodied context in which it is read.

Wolfe makes the case that this is a unique quality of fact-based New Journalism. To the contrary, I suggest the kind of readership that *In Cold Blood* requires might be adapted to all manner of media-generated virtuality. The remainder of this book seeks to build on this model of embodied media engagement, which depends on recognizing the overlapping virtual and material contexts in which media use takes place. To that end, the coming chapters explore incomplete worlds of narrative-based videogames, as they, too, stage our interactions with their virtual environments within broader social and cultural circumstances.

3 Incomplete Worlds

Videogames beyond Immersion

The excitement surrounding the immersivity of digital environments was in full force as Nintendo prepared to release its fifth-generation console, the Nintendo 64 (hereafter N64), in 1996. The signature launch title, *Super Mario 64* (developed by Nintendo EAD), incorporated this cultural desire to "step into" virtual reality into the game itself: to begin each level—or "world"—players must direct Mario to jump into a framed picture. This immersion metaphor appears in Nintendo's advertising campaigns for the game as well. In one television advertisement, running under the slogan "Change the System," Mario and his teenage companion backflip into a painting and then tour Mario's home world together.[1] Taking the plunge into this three-dimensional world was not as seamless as it appeared on television, however.

With its revolutionary free-roaming gameplay and a user-controlled dynamic camera, *Super Mario 64* invited players to explore a fully three-dimensional environment.[2] To implement these systems, Nintendo introduced several groundbreaking innovations in user interface; but, as discussed in the previous chapter, immersion requires a transparent interface. One of the more significant introductions was the dynamic camera system. Using the four yellow directional buttons, players could manipulate the view camera to their advantage, zooming in and out, rotating around Mario, fixing the camera to Mario or at any position in space. Being able to move the camera added to the impression of Mario's world as three-dimensional, freestanding

FIGURE 3.1. Mario jumps into a painting to start a new level in *Super Mario 64*.

space; but, at the same time, it draws attention to the player's mediated position relative to that space. The ability to move the camera introduced a tension between the player's role as Mario and as a media user. The player clearly cannot "be" Mario, running around Super Mario World butt-dropping Goombas, and be his cinematographer.[3] The very mechanics Nintendo developed to support immersive play thus presented significant obstacles to immersion.

To mitigate this issue, Nintendo attempts a narrative solution. The game incorporates the camera system into its fiction through the introduction of two new characters, the Lakitu Bros. One of these begoggled turtles seated in a flying cloud with a film camera hanging from a fishing rod arrives just as Mario is set to enter the Princess's Castle. He announces that *he* will be "filming the action live as [Mario] enters the castle and pursues the missing Power Stars" but proceeds to explain how *the player* can control the movement of the camera. Who, then, is doing the filming? According to the instruction manual, when the player manipulates the camera's viewing angle she does it "by controlling the Lakitu Bros," but that only compounds the problem. Switching between Mario's operator and his camera operators, the player can be neither.

The Lakitu Bros. exemplify an immersion-breaking issue that Jesper Juul calls the incoherence of videogame worlds. As Juul explains, fictional worlds are always incomplete because it "is not possible to specify all the details about any world."[4] As a result, most narrative-based games present "incoherent worlds, where the game contradicts itself or prevents the player from imagining a complete fictional world."[5] By introducing the Lakitu Bros., Nintendo expanded Mario's universe in an attempt to make narrative sense of its innovative camera interface. Even so, the fictional world remains incoherent. In order to explain the camera's control scheme, the Lakitu Bros. explicitly reference the four yellow arrow buttons on the awkward N64 controller.

According to Juul, in a complete, coherent world "it would make sense to assume that the characters in that world are generally unaware of their being fictional characters or being part of a game at all."[6] Therefore the Lakitu Bros. should not know anything about the player or the player's controller. When they mention the set of yellow buttons, they address the player not as Mario but as a machine operator. Despite an innovative dynamic camera that grants the player free exploration of a three-dimensional virtual world,

FIGURE 3.2. One of the Lakitu Bros. references the N64 controller as he explains how to change the camera angle in *Super Mario 64*.

that world remains incoherent and, thus, the player remains at the level of interface, sitting before a television screen, pressing yellow buttons on an oversized controller.

Rejecting the Immersive Fallacy

The field of videogame studies came together as an academic discipline at the tail end of the dot-com era. Even so, it admirably avoided the general fascination with the immersive potential of gaming's virtual worlds. Video-game studies joined the vanguard of digital and media studies responding to what N. Katherine Hayles called the "condition of virtuality" by affirming the material circumstances of our interactions with the virtual.[7] It had to be, given all the concern regarding the potential for impressionable young game-players to lose the ability to distinguish between reality and what they saw on-screen.

In *Rules of Play*, a foundational text for both videogame scholarship and development, Katie Salen and Eric Zimmerman coined the phrase "immersive fallacy" to describe the assumption that media should strive to present a fictional world so convincing that its audience would forget the real world in which they interact with the media.[8] Applying as much to attitudes about videogames as to first-generation VR, the immersive fallacy expects that eventually the technology will develop to the point that it will be able to effect a complete separation of media interface and virtual game world, such that users are in fact unaware that they are playing a game at all. Salen and Zimmerman point out, on the contrary, that games are fundamentally meta-communicative. They depend on the participants understanding and so remind them that they are involved in a game and in this game certain rules apply.

As Juul observes, creating massive car wrecks in *Burnout 2: Point of Impact* (Criterion Games, 2002) is only fun because it is a media-created event and the difference between the depicted crash and what it represents is never in question.[9] This logic extends to videogames of all sorts, and in chapter 7 I will suggest that even the much-maligned first-person shooter relies on its player recognizing that the waves of non-playable characters they will kill are only virtual representations. But this understanding also applies to the most advanced, hypothetically perfected VR simulator. Here, too, the experience of and interaction with the virtual environment is conditioned by the circumstances of engagement. If the sensory inputs of a VR system were so compelling that users truly believed that, after putting on a headset and glove, they were suddenly on the surface of the moon or on a battlefield in the Middle East, the experience would be utterly terrifying. Rather, the experience of the projected environment, no matter how successful the simulation, is framed by having moments earlier put on a VR headset or walked into a cave automatic virtual environment (better known as a CAVE). Even the members of the Starship *Enterprise* entered the perfected virtual worlds of the holodeck knowing they stepped into the holodeck and not the transporter.[10]

Videogame studies solidified as a discipline through the recognition that a fixation on the immersiveness of their environments missed the essential qualities of videogames as such. A group of scholars calling themselves "ludologists" carved out a space for videogame studies as a discrete area of study by shifting attention away from the allure of gaming's fictional worlds in order to analyze the distinctive formal, "ludic" properties of the medium.[11] Their pursuit of "video games' unique features as a form of expression" laid the groundwork for a medium-aware study of gaming and provided a critical vocabulary for a developing and increasingly influential cultural form.[12] However, while the ludologist arguments successfully subverted the immersive fallacy, they did so by assuming its hierarchical ontology.

The First Moves in Undermining Virtuality

I will not rehearse here the ludology/narratology debate, a conversation videogame scholars are surely tired of revisiting. I raise it here to discuss its ontological implications as exemplary of a kind of materialist response to the condition of virtuality spread in the dot-com era, which left the real/virtual binary intact by asserting the primacy of some "more real" element. The problem with this binary separation—independent of metaphysical issues—is that it produces a perception that the virtualities appearing on-screen are self-contained and reducible to the real world of hardware, code, and players. Virtual environments became more and more commonplace over the ludologist period, to the point that time spent in game worlds threatens to become an out-of-world economic concern.[13] Even so, under this model, they remain a second-order consideration, an inessential, even optional component.

Graham Harman uses the term "undermining" to describe the "claim that objects are unreal because they are derivative of something deeper."[14] It is, as Levi Bryant puts it, "the assertion of a fundamental strata of reality that constitutes the 'really real,'" which in turn discredits and ontologically devalues objects and phenomena not in that strata.[15] Though the tradition of treating games as ontologically undermined, or as if some component were "less real" than another, can be traced to the foundational approaches to the study of play, ludologist arguments in the late 1990s made it the cornerstone of the emerging field of videogame studies.[16] In his 2009 keynote address to the Digital Games Research Association annual conference, Ian Bogost charted the history of videogame studies through its attempts to answer the fundamental ontological question, what is a game? Though he didn't borrow Harman's term, Bogost made clear videogame scholarship's tendency toward undermining. What he calls the "first move in videogame ontology" belonged to the ludologists: "The formal structures of rules are real, and things like fictions and stories and the overall experience of those rules are byproducts to be found in the act of play, and in the minds of players."[17] As videogame studies came together as a field by defining its object of study, it did so on the foundation of the virtual/real binary, distinguishing the really real element of rules from the derivative element, fiction. Thus, rather than wholly refute the assumptions underlying the immersive fallacy, videogame studies reinscribed them.

Reproducing the Binary

Juul codified the ludologists' undermining binary in *Half-Real: Video Games between Real Rules and Fictional Worlds*. Juul's title refers to the double nature of videogames: "Video games are two rather different things at the same time: video games are real in that they are made of real rules that players actually interact with; that winning or losing a game is a real event. However, when winning a game by slaying a dragon, the dragon is not a real dragon, but a fictional one. To play a videogame is therefore to interact with real rules while imagining a fictional world and a videogame is a set of rules as well a fictional world."[18] While it might seem obvious, Juul makes an important distinction the required articulation given the hype surrounding computer-generated virtualities. Playing a game is a real event, even if the fictional environment it projects is only a representation ("the dragon is not a real dragon"). This is all correct. The undermining move, and where videogame studies has lost touch with virtuality, comes from the next step in saying that because the fictional is a representation it is derivative and inessential. The dragon may not be a dragon, but it is a projection of a dragon, and projections of dragons are real.

Indeed, fictional elements play an essential and very practical role in the "real" event of playing a game. On the one hand, videogames are a system of rule-based algorithms that determine what can be done in the game space and thus define how the game is played. The math in itself is not particularly entertaining and can be pretty abstract. So, on the other hand, videogames typically present themselves in the form of a narrative, which helps explain the rules and make the games more fun. In short, videogames are rules, skinned in human-readable representations. The narrative level works as an interface to the informatic level, teaching players the rules of the game through shorthand representations. A car in a game will likely have properties of real-life cars: it will be really heavy, capable of being driven, completely inedible, full of gas and potentially explosive, and so on. The fictional layer thus plays an important mediating function in gaming, recontextualizing the rules and joining them to systems of meaning and circuits of exchange beyond the screen.

Even so, for Juul—and many videogame scholars after him—fiction's role in gameplay suggests that narrative is really just an expression of the rules, a particular kind of formal element in the game's composition. Once the player has learned the shorthand, Juul explains, she can ignore the narrative all together and operate solely on the level of rules. It is, therefore, up to the player to decide "between imagining the world of the game and seeing the representations as a mere placeholder for information about the rules of the game."[19] In other words, the mediating fiction is optional.

Yet, even if the player choses to commit to the "fantasy" half of the game, they cannot truly escape the "real" half. As discussed earlier, Juul points out that the fictional worlds of videogames are necessarily incomplete and, thus, incoherent. As in the example with *Super Mario 64*, even as games become more graphically impressive, with smoother interfaces and more intuitive controls, they cannot describe every aspect of the projected reality, nor can they incorporate into the fiction every aspect of the player's interface with the gaming apparatus. Eventually a player will find a seam in the fabric of the virtual world, recognize that this is just a game, and return to the level of interface. Even more reason to discard the fictional.

Juul's characterization of the fictional environments of videogames as "incoherent worlds" demonstrates the debt videogame studies owes to the dot-com-era discourse surrounding immersion, even as it refutes the immersive fallacy. Juul even refers to Thomas Pavel on possible worlds theory and Marie-Laure Ryan's application of it to virtual environments (discussed at length in chapter 1) in his formulation of the concept. Videogames conjure fantastic, convincing fictional worlds, but they are incomplete, unable to cover over the user's "native" reality, and thus inessential.

Persistence of Undermining

Even as the field of videogame studies has moved on from ludology, the tendency toward undermining persisted. Bogost points out that each subsequent "move" in the ontology of videogames takes a basic undermining structure: "whatever a game is, some part of it is more real than another."[20] Whereas for the ludologists the reality of videogames is their rules of play, the last decade of videogame studies has, like the study of digital media in general, located the "really real" at all levels of substrata: code, hardware, platform, and practice. The result of these studies, however, has been to demonstrate just how multimodal and multifaceted videogames are. What was a binary has become a multiplicity. A videogame involves not only rules and narrative but the embodied experience of the user, the conditions of production, the social practices they generate, the material qualities of the hardware or platform, and so on. As Bogost puts it succinctly, "videogames are a mess." Rather than isolate the "really real" base on which to build an ontological hierarchy, the last decade of videogame studies has in fact demonstrated the inadequacy of any attempt to do so.

The "real event" of videogaming ripples across multiple, interwoven contexts—physical, social, virtual. Videogaming is, as Alexander Galloway puts it, a "unified, single phenomenon" even though it is a kind of "polyvalent doing," an action that occurs in several contexts simultaneously.[21] The platform executes code that forms the game that players receive via its interfaces, all transpiring within and in turn producing culture.[22] The rules defining the game are mediated by technologies presented to players in human-readable fictions, thereby enabling play within overlapping gamic and social spaces.[23] There is no single essential unit or hierarchy organizing the traditionally striated levels of videogaming's composition. They are interdependent yet belong to a flat ontology, each component layer engaging the others on equal ontological footing.[24] Mapping all the exchanges between layers initiated by playing a videogame would be impossible. Even so, meaningful claims about videogames—and new media in general—acknowledge and often have to trace trajectories that run across more than one layer or context.

Indeed, the field of videogame studies has started to get away from what Bogost calls "short-sighted essentialisms about computer hardware or human experience" and to expand the purview of what videogaming involves. Even so, the virtualities of fiction have remained a marginal element.[25] Videogame studies continues to be hesitant about the role of the fictional in gaming, perhaps as a result of the legacy of ludologist invectives against narrative, perhaps due to wariness of the immersive fallacy. Whatever the reason, the virtualities of game fictions continue to be subjugated to their material instantiation, collapsed into formal concerns or issues pertaining to composition, or discussed abstractly as in someway less than real. But, as Juul made clear, even as he undermined them, the virtualities of fiction play an important, "real" role in the polyvalent exchanges we call gaming. They re-skin technical operations, algorithmic calculations, and rule-based systems, recontextualizing them within systems of meaning and social practice. A code object, a set of commands scripted in an abstract, esoteric language, appears on screen as a car, and this technical operation is reframed in relation to the practice, experience, and culture of automobile travel. Playing in crash mode in *Burnout 2*, to return to Juul's example, our operation of a digital computing device becomes a way to "relate to death and disaster."[26]

Returning to Narrative

Part of the reason the fictional in gaming has been so easily undermined is the result of the concept of narrative typically applied to games. When the ludologists were defining the field by distinguishing gaming from storytelling, they wanted to be able to talk about rules and gameplay mechanics as separable and distinct from narrative. Set up to be set out, narrative was defined as linear, with a tightly controlled narrative arc, describing a self-contained, alternative world that isn't supposed to break the fourth wall.[27] It is no wonder, then, that games seem to offer their fictional worlds in only a "flickering, provisional, and optional way."[28]

But what if this issue is not that game worlds are incoherent, but with the expectation that they shouldn't be? What if the problem is with limitations in concept of fiction applied to them? After all, why would one expect twenty-first-century fiction to offer stable, coherent access?

Not only does this kind of definition foreclose anything like a videogame version of embodied readership discussed in the previous chapter, it is also a standard of narrative practice not expected of any other medium. Multiple, nested layers, internal incoherence, self-reference, and second-person address are frequent features of the last one hundred years of literary fiction (at least). Furthermore, given its relationship to hypertext literature and theory, video-game studies would seem to be well prepared to respond to nonlinearity, audience participation, and meta-media reference.[29] Yet it is precisely this kind of narrative complexity that videogame scholarship often has trouble addressing.

Gaming is, as Salen and Zimmerman remind us, inherently metacommunicative.[30] It requires that the players understand and acknowledge the terms, rules, and mechanics, and so depends on players recognizing, at some level, that they are indeed playing a game. Videogames are, in this sense, much like the nonfiction novel discussed in the previous chapter: the whole work proceeds from and is organized around the player's knowledge and aware-ness—going in and throughout—of the rules and circumstances. Even the most coherent game world would still necessarily be contextualized by a player's engagement with the machine and the game rules.[31] If games are by necessity metacommunicative in this way, always showing themselves to be incoherent—that is, referring back to the rules of play, the implementation media, and the player's interaction—then it makes little sense to expect them to be coherent and self-contained. Gaming requires players to discover and push the boundaries of a game's rule system, which is what makes them a fundamentally demystifying practice.[32] In that sense, gaming would seem to have more in common with literary metafiction than the abstract concept of self-contained fictional worlds.

Previous discussions of videogames in relation to contemporary literary techniques focus primarily on form.[33] As demonstrated in the prior chapter, metafiction implies more than formal considerations. Linda Hutcheon explains that metafiction operates through the recognition that "reading and writing belong to the processes of 'life' as much as they do those of 'art.'"[34] Incoherent self-reference in videogames works much the same way, opening a space to consider gaming as a "real event." The reader or player's self-aware engagement with the fictional brings the "incoherent" generated world in contact with the "real" world. Through self-reference, fiction meditates on its own place in the lived experience of its audience.

As I will discuss in chapter 5, bound up with the aesthetic, formal similarities, the emergence of videogames as a narrative medium coincident with the period of metafiction's literary dominance suggests that both respond to an emerging cultural trajectory. Indeed, both games and literary metafiction raise important questions about the relationship between art and life, media and mediation, and representation and responsibility, questions with increasing relevance given the ubiquity of virtual environments in the wired world. Yet videogames continue to be discussed as only "half real." In a culture defined by online banking, geotagged status updates, and augmented reality apps, binary ontological distinction makes little practical difference. The fictional worlds of videogames are incomplete to the extent they are interpenetrated with the supposedly "more real" realms of rules, code, hardware, platform, and practice. Their incoherence is an expression of the corresponsiveness of virtual and material contexts, which I call mixed realism.

Representational, art/life binary models are inadequate to the ways in which the artifice of gaming prompts and participates in the "life processes" of wired culture. Players engage the virtualities of game fictions, not as vicarious visitors to alternate virtual realities but as media users, for whom many everyday practices involve "artificial" environments. From this perspective, the interactive fictional worlds of videogames extend or update the paradoxes raised by literary metafiction. When cracks in the narrative façade cannot be ignored, the material circumstances of its implementation show through the gaps. However, rather than rendering these fictional worlds as merely optional diversions, their insufficiencies reveal points of interface and intersection between virtual and material contexts. They are, in this sense, self-reflexive, meta-media moments that reflect on the role of media-generated virtualities in the "real" media ecology.

Salen and Zimmerman lamented that the immersive fallacy has gotten in the way of videogame's developing as a self-reflexive art form: "Imagine the kinds of games that could result: games that encourage players to constantly shift the frame of the game, questioning what is inside or outside the game; games that play with the lamination between player and character, pushing and pulling against the connection through inventive forms of narrative play; games that emphasize metagaming, or that connect the magic circle so closely with external contexts that the game appears synchronous with everyday life."[35] They then turn from videogames in the last section of their argument to focus on alternative reality games as an example of the kind of ontological play they felt games might offer absent the industry's fixation on a certain version of immersivity. In the next chapter, I will demonstrate that the kinds of videogames Salen and Zimmerman imagine already exist if only we learn to interpret their incoherence as opening a space for self-referential engagement with the processes of life.

4 Gaming in Context

Self-Reflexive Strategies in *Prince of Persia:
The Sands of Time*, *Eternal Darkness:
Sanity's Requiem*, and *.hack//Infection*

Why does Mario have three lives?

Jesper Juul observes that Mario's three lives cannot be explained by the game's story about plumbers and princesses. As a result, without tacking on some undisclosed reanimation plot, we end up talking about rules in order to explain what is going on: "Mario is not reincarnated (fiction); the player just has three Marios (rules)."[1] For Juul, Mario's three lives exemplify the incoherence of videogame worlds. A game's narrative cannot explain everything. In this case, the rule governing how many tries the player gets to complete the game shows through. When it does, the fictional world of aggressive mushrooms and fiery castles collapses and the player returns to the "real" world where she is playing a videogame.

The lives system, however, was never intended as a narrative solution to maintain player immersion. It seems somewhat disingenuous and perhaps a little inappropriate to ask it to refer to the game's sparse story. Furthermore, the lives mechanic is not merely a function of the game rules but of their other "real" context, the video arcade.

As is well-known, the lives mechanic is a holdover economic solution to how to monetize gameplay in the pay-for-play context of the videogame arcade. Arcade videogames resemble midway or carnival games in their business model.[2] Flashing lights and attract loops fill the role of the carnival barker by attracting passersby to lay money down for the chance of overcoming a challenge. Just as a quarter at the carnival buys three throws at the dunk tank, a quarter at a *Pac-Man* kiosk buys three lives. In the arcade, this mechanic makes a lot of sense and a lot of money.

The pay-for-play model breaks the game into short, monetizable sessions. Each session does not require a huge investment in terms of time or money, but to see the entire game will cost multiple coins. The persistence of the lives mechanic, then, is not solely a matter of rules. It speaks more broadly to circumstances of play and to the range of contextual factors bearing on a player's interaction with the virtual world.

As one would expect, the correlation between rules and play environment dictated a change in the lives mechanic when console gaming brought videogames into the living room. A session of David Crane's *Pitfall!* (Activision, 1982), for example, designed for play on the Atari 2600, is set to a timer that counts down for twenty minutes. In that span of time, a player attempts to gather thirty-two pieces of treasure, which increase the final score, while avoiding hazards, which decrease her total. Organized into twenty-minute intervals, a session of *Pitfall!* is more like a television episode than a midway game kiosk. Nick Montfort and Ian Bogost observe that "in the arcade or the tavern, there is a social reason to limit gameplay, in addition to the financial incentive to increase coin-drop. But the living room invites people to consume media in much longer segments, such as the thirty-minute TV show."[3] Developed for home console play, *Pitfall!*, despite its inclusion of a lives system, was more amenable to the way people already consumed media, primarily television, at home.

These examples demonstrate that the incompleteness of videogame narratives reveals more than just the underlying rule systems they were meant to cover. In both the arcade and the home setting, the particular mechanism through which a game deals with the player's failure to complete the challenge becomes a rule of the game because of the circumstances in which players interact with the virtual. The rules that show through the cracks in the narrative surface are a material manifestation of embodied context bearing on the user's engagement with virtualities of the on-screen game world. Rather than the ontological foundation of gameplay, rules operate as a connecting node in a circuit joining on-screen and off-screen contexts.

When the rules or game mechanics appear in the gaps of game narratives it is a function of the terms of their exchange with the virtual world, which does not stand on its own either. In other words, if we stop expecting them to be ontologically opposed, we can start to understand how the virtual and the real interact, both with each other and with the player. The expectation that game narratives present coherent worlds implies the expectation that the virtualities of fiction and the real rules are self-contained and therefore separable. If we give up that binary, then the insufficiency of game worlds highlights points of intersection between on-screen and off-screen contexts. In this sense, the virtual worlds of videogames are incoherent only to the extent that they are inseparable from while irreducible to the social and material contexts in which we engage them.

This chapter will explore three games as they negotiate the tenuous task of positioning their players at the intersection of "real" and virtual environments. As Juul demonstrates, because the fictional worlds of videogames are necessarily incomplete, any non-diegetic element or element not covered by a narrative skin—such as the *Super Mario Bros.* lives mechanic, which is unable to incorporate player failure into the plumber's story—ruptures the projected world, exposing the material contexts of play. Ubisoft's *Prince of Persia: The Sands of Time* (2003), Silicon Knights's *Eternal Darkness: Sanity's Requiem* (Nintendo, 2002), and CyberConnect2's *.hack//Infection* (Bandai, 2002), however, attempt to circumvent this eventuality by writing typically non-diegetic elements *into* their stories.[4]

As in chapter 2 with *In Cold Blood*, this chapter also returns to a seminal moment in the understanding of media-generated virtualities—the burgeoning of videogames studies in the post-dot-com period—and attempts to chart an alternative trajectory by reading exemplary texts differently. In theory, these games solve the incoherence experienced in a game like *Super Mario Bros.* If potentially disruptive events like player failure, hardware failure, or simple menu operations are presented as part of the story, they do not refer the player back to the "real" world, thus allowing the player to stay immersed. Given that these games were all released shortly after the dot-com bubble had undeniably burst in 2001—when it was clear that videogames weren't the holodeck, home edition—promoting narrative coherence might have seemed like a way to compensate for videogaming's inadequacies as immersive media. However, rather than cover over their fault lines, these games expose them, engaging directly with the lived contexts in which they are played. Each game exhibits a self-reflexive, nested narrative that addresses players as media users. In doing so, they reference and incorporate into the space of play their own position within the "real" media ecology. Rather than rupture under incoherence, they *evert*, their fictions coextensive with the embodied circumstances of play. In this way, these games embrace mixed realism as central to their conceit and demonstrate how game fictions fold together real and virtual contexts.

Prince of Persia

Similarly to *Pitfall!*, Ubisoft's *Prince of Persia: The Sands of Time* attempts to promote continuity by responding to the material context of play. Near the end of the tutorial section the playable Prince discovers the Dagger of Time. When he presses a button on the Dagger's hilt—prompted by the player pressing a button on her controller—time moves backward and gameplay rewinds a few seconds. Functionally a do-over button, the Dagger of Time allows players to return to the point before a fatal error and try again. Should she miss a jump, get overwhelmed by monsters, or fall prey to a trap, a press of the button can return the Prince to the moments before his demise, allowing the player another chance.

Prince of Persia's signature replay mechanic keeps players engaged in the story world, even as they may struggle with the challenge of the game. As Juul's example of Mario's three lives exemplifies, player failure typically breaks

FIGURE 4.1. Pressing a controller button to activate the rewind mechanic prompts the playable Prince to press a button on the Dagger of Time in Ubisoft's *Prince of Persia*.

narrative continuity. Mario obviously cannot save the Princess if he falls to his death in World 1-3. The Dagger of Time dramatically cuts down how often this kind of rupture occurs and reduces the number of times the player encounters menus, save-game files, and loading screens. Similar to the timer in *Pitfall!*, the rewind mechanic is well suited to a home console environment. It lets the player press forward through the game despite potentially tiresome setbacks.

The game is not completely without challenge, however. The amount of time a player can rewind is limited by the amount of the dispersed Sands of Time she has collected. As a result, the player can be caught without enough of the Sands to take back a fatal error, and so the Prince still occasionally fails in his quest. To account for these player missteps, *Prince of Persia* employs another continuity measure, its nested narrative. Though it, too, addresses players in their lived environment as media users, the game's framing story also radically restructures the player's presumed relationship to the fictional world, denying them the role of the playable Prince.

At the game's climax, the Prince, distraught at discovering Princess Farah's lifeless body, thrusts the Dagger into a magical Hourglass filled with the accumulated Sands of Time. All the events that unfolded during eight or more hours of gameplay are reversed, as time runs backward to the moment before the adventure began. The Prince awakens in his camp outside the city walls and rushes to Farah's room before his father begins his invasion. Now a stranger to the Princess, he begins to tell her the story of the erased events, hoping to convince her to stop the traitorous Vizier's plot before it begins again.

The opening lines of his tale will sound familiar to the player, as they echo word for word the monologue spoken over the opening cutscene. The camera draws back to a view of Farah's balcony, which mirrors the establishing shot that served as background for the game's start menu. Moments earlier, the Prince paused to view Farah's balcony from the same vantage at which the player begins the game. The player's involvement begins not with the initial assault on the palace that comprises the game's tutorial section, but here, outside Farah's room and after the entire game has already occurred. With the first controllable action following the start screen, the Prince enters Farah's room to tell her everything that has already taken place.

FIGURE 4.2. On his approach to the palace to warn Princess Farah, the Prince pauses to view the veranda. The opening menu of Ubisoft's *Prince of Persia* starts from the same vantage point, suggesting that the player enters the story here, as the Prince prepares to tell Farah all that has already taken place.

The recurrence of elements from the game's opening sequences during the Prince's urgent return indicates that the player's run through *Prince of Persia* corresponds to the telling of the Prince's tale to Farah. Rather than conducting the Prince through events in the real time of their happening—his harrowing battles, narrow escapes, and witty comments—the player articulates the Prince's story from one cutscene to the next. However, if the playable Prince was telling a story for the duration of the game, what was the player doing? When she pressed buttons to interact with this virtual world, did she affect a fight with sand monsters or a detailed description of such a fight?

Through this frame story of the Prince as storyteller, *Prince of Persia* acknowledges its own storytelling. For example, when Farah challenges the veracity of his tale, the Prince admits, "You're right. It's just a story," conceding both that the events never took place and that our play-through amounts to spinning a fiction. Such self-conscious moments reflect back on the player's real-world position as audience to a digital narrative. As a result, however, the player cannot access the fictional world through the role of the Prince.

Prince of Persia uses this self-reflexivity to stretch its fiction over typically non-diegetic events. When the player initiates the quit-game sequence, for example, the narrator Prince implores, "Do you wish me to leave before finishing my story?" In this way, the player's non-diegetic action of interfacing with the menu takes on a narrative significance. If the player leaves, she risks the Vizier discovering the Prince before he has told the whole story. Thus, even her time away from the Prince's tale—that is, not playing *Prince of Persia*—has consequences within the game's fictional world. In this exchange, however, the player is positioned not as the playable Prince, but as his audience. Within the context of the narrative, the Prince's story is urgent; he certainly would not propose to leave. Further, the player was the one who moved to cut the story short, literally initiating what is called an interrupt in computer terminology when she presses the pause button. The Prince's reply—"As you wish"—thus places the player as the Prince's audience, namely, Farah.

But the player cannot take Farah's role either. The game's plot revolves around the interpersonal drama of two enemies who must trust each other to defeat their common betrayer, the Vizier, and save their respective people. This tension manifests in gameplay as environmental puzzles that require the characters to supplement each other's limitations so they may progress together. Though the Prince's acrobatics allow him to traverse the palace quickly, Farah knows its layout and can slip into areas that he cannot access by climbing. It is thus essential that the AI-controlled Farah be other and outside the playable role. So, if neither the Prince nor Farah, how is the player positioned to interact with this virtual world?

The frame narrative attempts to incorporate the extreme rupture of player failure into the fiction as well. Should the player run out the Sands of Time and allow the Prince to perish, the narrator chimes in, "No, no. That's not how it happened, let me start again." The Prince's comment recasts the player's failure into the tale-telling scenario; the Prince did not die, he was merely misrepresented. Because he is the one telling the story, however, his comment suggests he has misremembered his own death. Thus, even as the game recuperates this rift in its fictional world, it compromises the player's relationship

FIGURE 4.3. The Prince and Farah must rely on each other to navigate the palace in Ubisoft's *Prince of Persia*.

to the Prince. Indeed, it seems the player and Prince are engaged in different iterations of the story.

Prince of Persia is a videogame about storytelling, and as such it meditates on the nature of narrative in the digital age. Jason Rhody has argued that it exemplifies a "game fiction": "a progressive, ergodic, competitive narrative that is to be actualized by a player."[5] At the same time, by figuring the main playable character as the teller of a fantastic, looping story, *Prince of Persia* invokes the oral tradition of *One Thousand and One Nights*. The Prince's tale even retains the function Michel Foucault assigns to storytelling, indefinitely deferring the narrator's death ("No, no that's not what happened, let me start again").[6] In this context, Walter Ong reminds us that linear continuity is an "artificial [creation], structured by the technology of writing."[7] For primarily oral cultures, repetition and redundancy hold stories together, and coherence emerges through and depends on the exchanges between the speaker and an audience.

The teller–audience relationship in *Prince of Persia* is quite complex, expressed through the interweaving of narrative, game, and player. The Prince is simultaneously character, subject, interlocutor, and narrator of a story told

FIGURE 4.4. The Prince begins telling his story to Farah, echoing the monologue delivered as a voiceover to the game's initial cutscene in Ubisoft's *Prince of Persia*.

to the player but which the player articulates through gameplay. A full exploration of the oral tradition in *Prince of Persia* is beyond the scope of this treatment. Even so, through its invocation of the oral tradition, *Prince of Persia* positions the player within its fictional logic, not as an acrobatic Prince but as a media user in the complex, hybrid role of audience to an interactive digital narrative.

As stories in an oral culture are told again and again, by numerous tellers, innumerable times, each time a little differently, the Prince's tale is told—or played—over and over on digital software, by thousands of players, on multiple platforms, all over the world. Each individual play-through—completed in fits and starts as the player pauses, saves, fails, and restarts—recirculates the Prince's story, with its own subtle differences. The player thus need not play in the role of the Prince to be involved in the iteration and reiteration of his tale. Her interactive retelling completes its invocation of the oral tradition, updated for a twenty-first-century media ecology.

Likewise, the game's signature rewind mechanic addresses the player within her lived context as a media user in a digital culture. The Dagger of Time orients gameplay around time management: has the player preserved enough time to finish the story? The player can rewind gameplay only if she has collected enough of the Sands of Time from around the palace. Having and using a rewind at the right time is a crucial strategic element of the game. For example, should the player make a mistake just after saving her progress, it may not be worth the expenditure of Sands to rewind. With bigger battles and more trying traps on the horizon, it may be better to reload a previous save point. The ability to rewind becomes more valuable the longer the player goes without saving. Should the player get caught without enough Sands at the end of a long battle or just before the next save point, she will lose her progress and have to start the session over. Conserving the Sands, then, simultaneously helps preserve the Prince's life as well as the player's time investment.

The challenge of games on the home console has largely shifted away from whether the player has the requisite skill to complete them to whether she has the requisite time. *Super Mario Galaxy* (Nintendo EAD, 2007) still features a lives mechanic but offers extra lives so freely that losing them is inconsequential. The 2008 HD-console *Prince of Persia* reboot eliminates the rupture of player failure altogether, as Farah's replacement, Elika, simply saves the Prince every time he falls. The player could play through the entire story, start to finish, without interrupting the narrative, provided, of course, she has enough time and attention. Such an expectation, however, would be unrealistic.

When *The Sands of Time* and its rewind mechanic came out in 2003, the dot-com bubble had undeniably burst and attention was being called "the new currency of business."[8] With the proliferation of easily accessible content and platforms on which to consume it, attention has become the precious commodity of the information age. In this context, *Prince of Persia's* nested narrative and rewind mechanic have as much to do with promoting cohesion as with simply keeping the player engaged. Each rupture introduces the possibility that the player might find other ways to spend her time.

In a literal sense, the Prince's urgent pleas to continue his tale *are* spoken to the player. When the Prince falls, he demands immediately to start his story again. When the player moves to quit, the Prince implores her to let him finish. In these moments, the game appeals to the player neither as the Prince, nor Farah, nor any other fictional character, but as a media user within a digital attention economy. For her, playing a videogame is merely one ordinary life process among others.

Eternal Darkness

Silicon Knights's *Eternal Darkness: Sanity's Requiem* also sets up its signature game mechanic to engage with the player as media user. Its patented "sanity effects" explicitly reference and incorporate typically non-diegetic machine actions into the game. While this should break the coherence of the fictional world, it effectively extends to involve the broader, real-world media ecology. In this way, *Eternal Darkness* exceeds the limits of the on-screen display and interacts with the off-screen world of the player.

Along with a health and magic bar, playable characters also have a sanity bar that indicates how well the character is keeping it together. The character loses sanity in a variety of scenarios such as entering a room full of zombies, getting injured, or witnessing something horrific in a cutscene. If a character's sanity bar gets low enough, a sanity effect is triggered.

These effects take a multitude of forms and ratchet up in severity as the character's sanity wanes. At first, they manifest as changes in the environment, such as distortions of space, constant screams and crying in the background, and blood running down the walls. More significant losses result in abrupt interruptions of the game. These are often triggered as a character leaves one room and moves into another. They typically present to the character something they want, like extra weapon ammo, or something they fear, like a room full of tough zombies.

Many of the sanity effects are context specific, relating to a particular character at a particular time in a particular setting: Alex discovers her own body bled out in the bathtub; Max flashes to his cell in the insane asylum; a character who has a shotgun finds ammunition for it. The effects can be more or less intense and are often quite surreal. For example, a character can enter a room and immediately explode into a pile of blood or find his head lying on the floor several feet in front of him as he ambles around before being made whole again when the effect wears off. When this happens the screen will flash and the character will reappear at the room's entrance as if nothing had happened. Coming out of these visions, every character, on every occurrence, exclaims, "This isn't happening!"

Context-specific effects are not limited to the world of the playable characters but also transpire in the context of the player's interaction with the game. Along with blood flowing down the walls, a mild sanity effect has common houseflies of various sizes skitter across the screen as if on the player's monitor. Sanity effects such as these refer to the player's environment and the implementation media by which they interact with the virtual world. The simulation of houseflies on the screen is not, then, a representation of the playable character's state of mind but an illusion directed specifically at people watching the playable character on a monitor.

Other effects simulate unintended monitor operations. The screen can also go instantly blank, as if the screen had been turned off or the power had gone out, or it might display only "video" in the upper right-hand corner, as if the monitor had lost its video input or switched to a different video channel. Sanity effects will change the in-game volume, turning it up while displaying the common green text of a television volume control interface or shutting it off completely with "mute" in green text displayed in the upper right.

None of these effects rightly have anything to do with the mental state of the playable characters. Instead, *Eternal Darkness* mobilizes the gaming

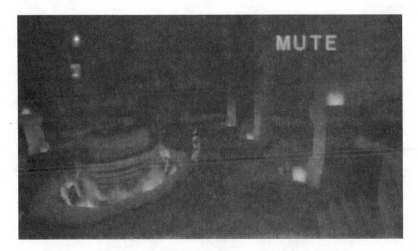

FIGURE 4.5. This "sanity effect" suggests that the player's television has been muted in Silicon Knights's *Eternal Darkness*.

media apparatus itself as a playable, fictional element. When the game simulates these television operations, the television itself is the object of the player's concern. In short, *Eternal Darkness* puts the player's television into play.

Instead of drawing the player in, these sanity effects extend the virtual world into the player's real-world space, incorporating the media itself into the fiction. *Eternal Darkness* uses reference to the media and the player's context to simulate events that would have immediate and real consequences for the player. Switching the video input, muting the volume, or other such play with the display, for example, may convince the player to check the settings on her television. These media-aware events have no bearing on the playable character, who, like Juul's Mario, is in no position to know about their own digital display. They apply to and have consequence for the *player* alone.

This is particularly apparent when the sanity effects involve non-diegetic player actions such as saving a game. One of the more insidious sanity effects changes the text on the save-game menu, giving the player the option to either delete all saved game data or continue without saving. Regardless of which menu option the player selects, the game appears to delete all save files. The playtime on *Eternal Darkness* is substantial, especially considering

FIGURE 4.6. In this "sanity effect" in Silicon Knights's *Eternal Darkness* the player is asked whether she wants to delete saved game data and then, regardless of the selected option, the game pretends to delete it.

the three play-throughs required to finish the entire story. Moreover, *Eternal Darkness* can be quite a difficult game and saving at regular intervals is often the only way to make progress. When a sanity effect makes it look like a saved game has disappeared, it has a direct impact on the player who thinks, even for a moment, that her hours of progress have been lost.[9]

The save menu is the quintessential non-diegetic player action, meaning it is an aspect of gaming unrelated to narrative concerns but which the player performs to configure play. It therefore has nothing to do with the game's story about Ancients and chosen and zombies. Further, this anxiety does not involve imagining oneself in the role of a playable character. Even so, the simulation of data deletion extends sanity effects into this non-diegetic region, making it diegetic as well. The fear of having lost a significant investment of time and effort in a videogame is of concern only outside the screen and primarily to the player who has logged those hours. In this way, these media-aware sanity effects prey on the player's immediate and very real investment in the game.

In another particularly disruptive effect, the screen will turn blue and display text in a computer font, claiming a fatal exception error in simulation of what is known in computing circles as the "blue screen of death." This sanity effect attempts to convince the player the console itself is broken. If this were

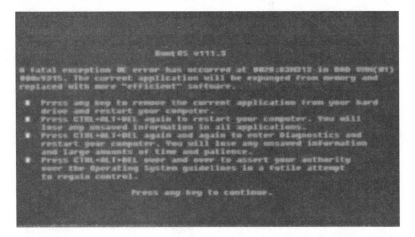

FIGURE 4.7. This "sanity effect" in Silicon Knights's *Eternal Darkness* simulates a fatal system error, suggesting the player's game console may be broken.

an actual "blue screen of death," the player would have lost her progress and may need to repair or purchase a new GameCube.[10]

Another example pushes the circle of play out even further. Upon completing a level in the middle of the game, a still screen announces that the story continues in an upcoming sequel, *Eternal Darkness: Sanity's Redemption.* The suddenness of this seeming conclusion—with no resolution in sight—likely provokes confusion and even outrage in the player. Has there been some mistake? Did I purchase the wrong disc? Have I been shortchanged, ripped off? Is this some new cynical plan by game distributors to get me to pay twice to get the full game? Now how will I know how the game ends?

A few moments later, the sequel screen disappears and the game continues as usual. Just another sanity effect. Beyond the player's gaming setup, television, console, or even software, this effect situates players within gaming culture and the gaming industry more broadly by invoking cycles of advertising and release. In reality, there was no sequel and, after a series of legal disputes that further contextualize the player's encounter with this sanity effect, there will not be one.[11]

Even though they are not "real"—the machine has not crashed, there is no sequel—these sanity effects threaten the player in a way that the game's zombies do not because of the way the narrative has positioned its audience as media users. They manipulate directly the player's relationship to the game, making that media relationship itself the site of play. *Eternal Darkness* denies players the opportunity to "play as" its characters by foregrounding their interaction with the media in such a way that we can only "play as" the game's player. Our real-world interaction with the controller, our television, our save data, even our ownership of the full game, become diegetic elements.

This player-as-player perspective changes the status of in-game elements as well. Recall that many sanity effects appear to be relevant only to the playable character experiencing them. When Dr. Lindsay, for example, finds extra shotgun shells, they would be of use only to him because he has a shotgun, and therefore when the effect wears off and they disappear it is only he who is disappointed they are gone. From the perspective of the player, however, those shotgun shells, though not real ammunition, do aid in the completion of the game. Ammunition is particularly scarce in the game and finding a store of them would be exciting for any player struggling through a difficult level.

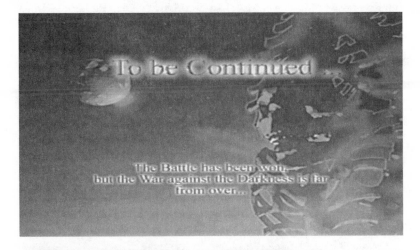

FIGURE 4.8. This "sanity effect" in Silicon Knights's *Eternal Darkness* attempts to convince the player that the game has concluded and will be continued in an upcoming sequel.

When they disappear and the player is disappointed, it is not that she has identified with Lindsay and feels bad for him that he will not have the benefit of shotgun shells; rather, the player is disappointed that she herself will not have the advantage of powerful ammunition in the game. Likewise, when Alex enters the hallway to find a horde of zombies, those zombies threaten the player's ability to succeed. Just about all the sanity effects, then, even the ones specific to a playable character's context, bear on the player's investments in playing the game and thus apply to the player context as well. In other words, every sanity effect—both diegetic (shotgun shells, zombies, etc.) and non-diegetic (save files, TV settings, sequels, etc.)—address the player as such.

It might appear that this diegetic inclusion of the player's lived context comes at the cost of the narrative itself. Viewing *Eternal Darkness* through the lens of the player's role as player would seem to institute a similar ontological divide as appeared in the ludology arguments. The narrative of *Eternal Darkness*, however, much like that of *House of Leaves* (discussed in chapter 6), has written the user's role as a user into the story itself.

Eternal Darkness, the videogame, presents itself as the new media manifestation of the flesh-bound *Tome of Eternal Darkness*. As such, it facilitates awareness and exchange between multiple, "separate but simultaneous"

FIGURE 4.9. Playable protagonist Alex Roivas in Silicon Knights's *Eternal Darkness* accesses the timestreams of another "chosen" by reading from the *Tome of Eternal Darkness*.

FIGURE 4.10. In Silicon Knights' *Eternal Darkness*, upon discovering the room in which her ancestor, the colonial-era Max Roivas, killed his house servants, Alex experiences a "sanity effect" as their timestreams momentarily overlap.

timestreams, both in-game and out-of-game.[12] Just as the playable Alex enters the battle against the Ancients by picking up the mystical book, players of the game *Eternal Darkness* continue the struggle against their eternal return with their multiple plays through the digital game. When Alex starts a new chapter of the *Tome* and skips across timestreams to embody another chosen, the player starts a new level of the game and assumes a new avatar. The player's implementation apparatus—the console, controller, television, in-game menus, interfaces, and so forth—thus all belong and are consistent with the game's story of mediated engagement across timestreams. Even potentially world-rending events—such as the player allowing their avatar chosen to perish—fits in this fictional conceit. Though the chosen's defense against the Ancients fails in one timestream, the player need only load up the game again to enter a new one where they might succeed.

Of course, there is nothing "true" about the mythology of the Ancients, the undead monsters, or the cosmic battle across time and space to preserve the balance of the universe. Even so, the fictional events are conducted in and through the gaming hardware and the player's position as a media user. Because the game situates the player as the next chosen, destined to continue the battle against the Ancients through a videogame, as Alex did through the *Tome*, reference to the gaming apparatus, rules, non-diegetic menu operations, and so on do not so much reveal the incompleteness of the game world as they extend that world beyond the limit of the screen. Thus, even though the world of *Eternal Darkness* is undeniably fictional, it is also inseparable from the player's interaction with the media.

.hack//Infection

One of the more extreme examples of a game addressing its players in their real-world circumstances as media users is CyberConnect2's *.hack//Infection*. Billed on its packaging as a "simulated MMORPG: no internet connection required!" *Infection* is the first in a series of four single-player, offline games conducted through the representation of a massively multiplayer online role-playing game called *The World*.[13] Players take the role of a new player of *The World*, making *Infection* a videogame in which one plays a videogame.

This positioning begins with the player completing user registration for *The World*. She enters her own username, which never appears again, and a

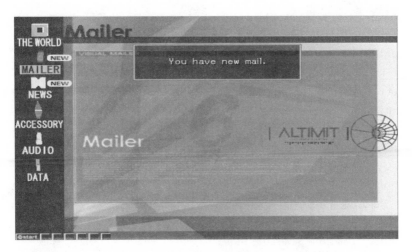

FIGURE 4.11. The desktop interface of the ALTIMIT OS in CyberConnect2's *.hack// Infection*.

character name, "Kite" by default. Then a simulated BIOS boots the made-up ALTIMIT operating system (OS) that opens to a desktop, displaying icons for programs and system settings such as "The World," "Mailer," "News," "Accessory," "Audio," and "Data."

Functioning as the main menu of the game, the ALTIMIT desktop confronts the player as if she were sitting before a screen, ready to click on an icon and boot up a videogame, which of course she is.[14] Setting it apart from other games in which the playable character is digital-media user, *Infection* has no playable characters outside the virtual environment of *The World*.[15] There is an authored character for the player to "play as," who goes by the in-*World* character name "Kite" and occasionally says something. Kite's user, however, is never seen and never taken on as a playable character. It is only when signed into *The World* that we get an avatar character to play around with and fight monsters. Out of *The World* there is no avatar, only the ALTIMIT desktop.

It is as if a layer of mediation between us and the virtualities of *Infection* has been removed. Rather than adopting an authored character as an extension of ourselves for the purposes of navigating the virtual environment and interacting with the fiction, we engage directly with many elements such as the desktop, the bulletin boards, the Mailer program, and *The World*'s sign-in screen. Even when we do adopt an avatar, *Infection* does not position us *as* Kite, but as a videogame player who interfaces with *The World* through Kite. The player's relationship to Kite, then, is the same in both the context of the narrative and the context of videogame-playing. Kite is not *virtually* an avatar or a *fictional* avatar; Kite simply *is* an avatar. Likewise, the player of *Infection* need not imagine herself to be in a virtual world or adopt a fictional role because simply by taking up the controller she already *is* a videogame player. In this way, *Infection* superimposes the player's role in the game's fiction onto her real-world role as a person interacting with a console.

Infection solves many of the problems of an incoherent game world, since any reference to the console medium, to control schemes, to game rules and procedures, game saves, the whole gaming apparatus and practice, extend the narrative. The simulated ALTIMIT desktop operating system transforms the typically non-diegetic main-menu interface into a playable diegetic space. The tutorial, which introduces the player to the game's control scheme by making explicit reference to buttons and menus, does not break the narrative either. While it may seem odd that Mario would be aware of the buttons

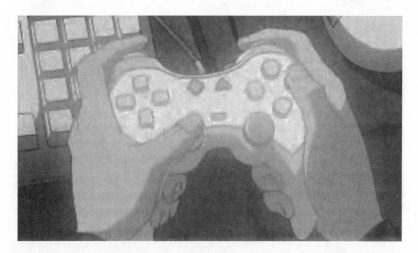

FIGURE 4.12. The controller used to play *The World*, as it appears in Koichi Mashimo and Masayuki Yoshihara's *.hack//Liminality, Vol. 1: In the Case of Mai Minase*—an anime DVD packaged with CyberConnect2's *.hack//Infection*—resembles a white Playstation2 controller.

on a GameCube controller, there is no such problem for *Infection*. When the non-playable character Orca mentions the buttons on a PlayStation2 controller, he is playing the same game with the same interface. *Infection* doesn't even need to explain player failure or its lives mechanic. Kite is a videogame avatar; when it dies, it just respawns.

Rather than trying to make the fictional world coherent enough to block out the player's real-world interaction with the media and the game, *Infection* makes the narrative about gaming itself. It thereby uses the player's real-world interaction as the very site of the fiction. As a result, it extends beyond the screen to aspects of being a gamer that do not transpire in-game.

The game of *The World* does not comprise the entirety of the *Infection* universe; it is just one of several computer programs. The rest of *Infection*'s world is implied through simulation of other communication media: a newsfeed reader, e-mail, and bulletin boards. The player's access to the larger fictional world, of which *The World* is part, becomes available through the channels available to any computer user, encountered only as electronic transmissions.

Being a videogame player does not mean one does nothing but play videogames all day. As Orca reminds the player at the beginning of the game, "People do have a life, you know. We're not online 24/7." Players take breaks,

FIGURE 4.13. The player's avatar, Kite, remarks on the difference between his friend, Yasuhiko, and Yasuhiko's avatar, Orca, in CyberConnect2's .hack//Infection.

go to work or school, have families, and maintain hobbies besides gaming. As a result, the fictional gamer characters in *Infection* are not always in-*World*, and so are not always available to join the player's party. At one point in the story, for example, Mistral leaves the group abruptly when the (fictional) gamer playing her must hurry to salvage her burned dinner.

Infection makes a point of including the out-of-*World* lives of its characters in its narrative in ways that influence gameplay. In doing so, it opens a place in its fiction for the off-screen lives of its own players. Because *Infection* positions players in the role of videogame players, all the operations, events, and realities associated with being a gamer, instead of breaking the spell of a fictional world, corroborate its (virtual) reality. Pausing the game to get a drink from the kitchen fits within our role. Thus the real soda the player retrieves from her real fridge is *in the game*. In fact, one never even has to pick up a controller to be a part of a reality in which millions of people play the videogame played in *Infection*. *The World* already belongs to our world. Synchronizing the player's actual role engaging the media with the role she plays in the story, *Infection* effectively integrates itself into the everyday reality of its players.

As a result, *Infection* places players in a position of risk in a way that the player of Rockstar North's *Grand Theft Auto IV* (Rockstar, 2008) does not expose its players to getting shot. At the end of the tutorial section, Orca takes Kite into dungeon to practice his new skills. They soon encounter a monster, Skeith, who uses a mysterious special attack to kill Orca. Kite escapes, logs out of *The World*, and discovers that, following Skeith's attack, Orca's operator in the real world, Yasuhiko, has fallen into a coma. For the rest of the game, the player guides Kite on a quest to discover what has happened to his friend. Now, the fictional "data drain" that afflicted Orca and numerous other characters does not exist and does not threaten to render the player of *Infection* comatose. However, simply by picking up the controller, the player becomes a digital media user, subject to a host of real-world concerns. Through its fictional conceit, *Infection* invokes these concerns and folds them back onto the act of play.

The *.hack* franchise is broadly about the potential dangers of an increasingly digitized culture. *Infection* takes place in 2010, five years after a prepubescent hacker caused network-wide system failures, which resembled the predicted effects of Y2K. Pluto's Kiss, as this cyber disaster was called, affected every computer not running ALTIMIT. Most then believed ALTIMIT was impervious to viruses, leading to near-universal adoption of the OS and a dramatic escalation of the threat posed if a new virus managed to infect it. Perhaps the most serious effect of the Pluto's Kiss incident was the arming of the world's automatic-response nuclear defense systems, putting the planet at risk of mutually assured destruction. When the virus Kite and company encounter in *The World* starts putting users into comas and causing blackouts, media outlets declare a new cyber disaster, Pluto Again.

Of course, in reality, Pluto's Kiss did not take place; no hacker shut down the entire Internet, potentially triggering a nuclear holocaust. Even so, even though it didn't happen, can we really call such a threat fictional? Y2K did not take place either, yet the potential is certainly there. In 2010, the year in which *Infection* takes place, a clock malfunction disabled millions of PlayStation3 consoles for a full day.[16] Around that same time Microsoft's Windows operating system owned a 90 percent market share. Did we not share similar risks as the ALTIMIT users?[17] Paul Virilio has written at length about the automatic weapons defense systems as potentially becoming so fast in response that they remove the human decision making from the equation.[18] Might we be in a similar scenario as the one described in the game, in which a computer malfunction could trigger nuclear apocalypse without and before human intervention? Moreover, the Internet will likely be the next battlefront, as a well-placed cyberattack could have catastrophic effects. In 2010 the United States was already preparing for this eventuality, playing at cyberattack war games—intended to be "quite realistic"—which they simultaneously aired on television for public consumption.[19] The United States already uses malware as a part of its military strategy.[20] Are large-scale, weaponized computer viruses really that far off?

It is in these "real world" contexts that *Infection* situates its players, much more so than its admittedly and unavoidably incomplete fictional world. With these real possibilities as consequences of the ubiquity of digital technologies in everyday life, picking up a controller to play a digital game like *Infection* isn't much of an escape. Because videogaming takes place in the real world, what happens in videogames takes place in the real world as well and cannot be isolated from outside-the-game occurrences, experiences, and values.[21] Edward Castronova has demonstrated how participating in the fictional gold economy in Verant Interactive's *Everquest* (989 Studios, 1999) is to participate in the actual global economy.[22] The virtualities of *Infection* do not have the same real-world efficacy as the gold economy in *EverQuest*; *Infection* isn't even an online game. Even so, it positions its players as really and truly digital media users, plugging them into the digital media ecology and all that comes with it.

This is what I call mixed realism, the continuity created by the exchanges between fictional events and the material circumstances. No matter how fantastic or incoherent, media-generated virtual realities are inextricably "mangled"—to borrow Constance Steinkuehler's term—with the supposedly more "real" component layers implementing them.[23] In short, videogames are real life. Acknowledging that fact and avoiding the kinds of "short-sighted essentialisms" described in the previous chapter require the recognition that interactions with fictional virtualities are a "part of life experience."[24]

Indeed, these three games do not merely represent or metaphorize contemporary wired culture, they *enact* it. To play *Prince of Persia* participates in the evolution of the storytelling tradition within an attention economy. To play *Eternal Darkness* makes one vulnerable to hardware failure and the politics and economics of release cycles. To play *.hack//Infection* places one within a wired culture in which cyberterrorism is an omnipresent threat. These self-reflexive games expose complex articulations of social, cultural, and material realms in relatively unmediated form overlapping the player's immediate act of play in virtual environments. In this way they engage important questions about the relationship between art and life, the virtual and the real. While this is somewhat easier to notice in games explicitly about digital media and culture, mixed realism can be seen at work whenever a game opens an opportunity for players to recognize a relationship between what is happening on-screen and real-world circumstances bearing on play.

Prince of Persia ends with Farah asking the Prince, "Why did you invent such a fantastic story?" After a failed (and rewound) attempt at romance, the Prince accepts that their adventure is now merely a fiction. But both the Prince and the player know something took place, even if all that remains is the telling. Such paradoxes will define our mixed reality. The next chapters discuss what is at stake in our responses to them.

5 Metafiction and the Perils of Ubiquitous Mediation

Though the dream of fully immersive, sensory-replacing virtual reality greatly influenced the cultural understanding of digitally generated virtual environments, the VR paradigm does not describe our typical, everyday interactions with these nonphysical spaces. This is particularly apparent in the contemporary period, in which virtual environments play a role in even the most mundane daily activities.

A simple example occurs when I use a map application on my smartphone to look up the location of a restaurant. I orient myself to the physical world around me by checking my location relative to the restaurant on a digital map. While doing so, the two-dimensional street map drawn on the handheld screen does not "replace" the physical world, submerging me in a "virtual reality." The ontology of the virtual map relative to the phone, the restaurant, or me, the user, does not factor into this exchange at all. The virtual works in concert with the real, augmenting my ability to orient myself through a mixture of virtual and material elements.

This scenario resembles much more closely the recent technical paradigm of mixed reality. Mixed reality arose out of and in response to what Mark Hansen calls the "clichés of disembodied transcendence as well as the glacial pace of progress in head-mounted display and other interface technology" associated with the first-generation of VR research.[1] Hansen describes the difference as follows: "Rather than conceiving the virtual as a total technical

FIGURE 5.1. The Monocle feature of the Yelp app for iPhone uses the device's camera to insert placards for local restaurants into the physical environment. Pictured here is the popular Freret Corridor near my home university in New Orleans.

simulacrum and as the opening of a fully immersive, self-contained fantasy world the mixed reality paradigm treats it as simply one more realm among others that can be accessed through embodied perception or enaction."[2] Whereas the VR paradigm presumes an opposition between virtual and material environments, the mixed reality paradigm acknowledges "the fluid interpenetration of realms."[3] Successful mixed reality interfaces still depend on minimizing the dissonance when moving between contexts, albeit not as a way to fool or replace "natural" stimulation. Instead, as in the example of the map application above, subjects interact with and between computer-generated and the relatively unmediated as co-constituents of the same environment.

Scenarios such as this one, in which the integration of real and virtual expand the horizon of embodied interactions, are increasingly common-place in contemporary wired culture. Display screens—big and small—touch interfaces, and, soon, wearable computing and nanotechnologies penetrate nearly all aspects of daily life. As a result, Machiko Kusahara claims that mixed reality "will soon become a key concept in understanding the world today where the reality is so often mixed with virtuality."[4] If indeed "all reality is mixed reality" as Mark Hansen claims, where does literary fiction fit in this paradigm?[5]

The place of print novels in a mixed reality has received little attention, and nothing like the explosion of criticism comparing literature to develop-ments in virtual reality discussed in chapter 1. The contemporary media ecol-ogy potentially signals a new role for readers under a mixed reality paradigm. Even though literary fiction is often considered to be in competition with digital media, print technology—just like VR and videogames—can gener-ate media-dependent virtual environments as well. The mixture of virtual and real in the contemporary processes of life thus rightly includes literary fiction. Moreover, Kusahara argues that acknowledging "the continuity and equality between real and virtual worlds" can help us to "recognize and deal with different types of fictional, imaginary, non-physical space we conceive in our daily life, and locate them in the physical space around us."[6] How do we understand the "fictional" in such a context, where virtuality itself, not just the medium of implementation, is the foundation of real-life expe-riences? How does the "fictional" integrate with the "realities" of everyday life? How do the imaginary on-screen entities influence and interact with off-screen social practices? Can the virtualities of fiction become, as did *Super Columbine Massacre RPG!* (Danny Ledonne, 2005), "frighteningly visceral"?

Metafiction in a Mixed Reality

The literary fiction contemporary with the development of digital technologies and VR interfaces doesn't much resemble the realist novels of the nineteenth century. While Ivan Sutherland was creating the first head-mounted display, Ralph Baer was building the first home videogame console, and Marshall McLuhan was pondering media's message, the literary avant-garde—exemplified by authors such as Thomas Pynchon, Robert Coover, and John Barth—was experimenting with alternative histories, pop-culture references, decentered narratives, and self-reflexive irony. Indeed, the postmodern aesthetic that tracks with the expansion of televisual and digital communication technologies in the later half of the twentieth century self-consciously rejected the values of literary realism and adopted techniques that would "pose questions about the relationship between fiction and reality."[7] In the midst of rapid proliferation of media-generated virtualities that would take us from the introduction of all-color television broadcasting to the dot-com crash in approximately fifty years, engineers and authors alike concerned themselves with the fluid ontological boundary between the artificial and the actual.[8]

The seeming rejection of realist aesthetics stirred objections from literary critics. Self-reflexive, metafictional techniques, it was often argued, turned art's gaze inward on itself, and thereby "severed completely or resolutely denied . . . the life–art connection" practiced by the realist tradition.[9] Alternatively, in her comparisons of literary techniques and immersive digital technologies, Marie-Laure Ryan places metafiction squarely on the side of life, foregoing the fictional altogether. "By overtly recognizing the constructed, imaginary nature of the textual world," metafiction, she argues, "reverts to the status of *nonfictional* discourse about non-actual possible worlds" (emphasis added).[10] Metafiction thus cuts itself off from the "real world" by addressing its own place within it.

Defenders of so-called narcissistic narratives responded that these metafictions constitute a reformation of the mimetic tradition through this seeming paradox. According to Linda Hutcheon, metafictional practices engage in "process mimesis," conscripting readers in an open-ended process of story-telling.[11] This "new role for readers," however, confronts them with a contradiction: "On the one hand, [the reader] is forced to acknowledge the artifice, the 'art,' of what he is reading; on the other, explicit demands are made upon him, as a co-creator, for intellectual and affective responses comparable in scope and intensity to those of his life experience. In fact, these responses are shown to be part of his life experience."[12] Metafiction owns up to the constructedness of its virtualities, yet it takes "nontrivial effort" to engage with them.[13] Readers must acknowledge significant intellectual and affective interactions with something they know all along is artificial. Because it enacts the fictional as a source of actual life experience, Hutcheon describes reading metafiction as paradoxical. But that was before the Internet became a household technology.

In the contemporary age of ubiquitous digital communication technologies, Hutcheon's paradox is a way of life. "We live in 'real' environments that are flooded with 'unreal' images," writes Kusahara.[14] They can be "seen everywhere, from regular TV screens to extra large screens on the street corner or to mini-screens on mobile phones, mixing the real and the virtual, the close and distant."[15] With the rise of the Internet, the spread of mobile phone use, and the proliferation of social networking services, as well as the popularity of videogaming, everyday life is suffused with telepresent interactions in virtual spaces, material effects of virtual communications, and media-dependent constructions. Moreover, we tend to think of these technologies less as tools than as environments we inhabit, (cyber)spaces where significant and, just as important, banal social interactions occur.[16] Digital virtualities are so imbricated in the practice of daily life in networked society that attempting to meaningfully distinguish between synthetic and "real" experiences is not only untenable; as Edward Castronova puts it, "our culture has moved beyond the point where such distinctions are helpful."[17]

The paradoxical perspective Hutcheon describes may be resolved by the mixed reality paradigm. Much like metafiction, a mixed reality paradigm practices an integration of virtual and real contexts rather than attempting to impose distinct ontological categories. Hansen argues that in mixed reality, "real" ceases to be taken as a property of discrete phenomena, as "emphasis falls less on what is perceived in the world than on how it comes to be perceived in the first place."[18] Or, in Hutcheon's terms, the mixed reality paradigm shifts focus from convincing *products* to interactive *processes*. Whereas for Hutcheon real experiences of the virtualities of media still seem like a paradox, for Hansen that tension dissolves in "the convergence of physical and virtual spaces informing today's corporate and entertainment environments."[19] Thus, within a mixed reality context, metafiction takes on its own kind of *realism*.

Metafiction thus has potential as a model for understanding the comingling of the artificial and the actual that defines our increasingly mixed reality. By inviting its audience to not only reflect on but also participate in fiction as an interactive, real-world process, metafiction can help us "locate," as Kusahara would say, the "fictional, imaginary, and non-physical space in our daily lives."[20] Yet this kind of "realism" is not without its perils.

The Trouble with Self-Reflexive Realism

Already by 1992, the author David Foster Wallace was arguing that metafictional realism's critical capacities had been compromised. In "E Unibus Pluram," Wallace recognized the mimetic qualities of mediation as tied to the expansive and expanding role of virtual media in daily life. Rather than subvert the "canonical cinctures of narrative and mimesis," Wallace argues, metafiction constitutes "a natural adaptation of the hoary techniques of literary realism to a nineties world whose defining boundaries have been deformed by electric signal."[21] Yet, writing on the cusp of the dot-com boom, for Wallace it wasn't the ubiquity of digital technologies blending media-generated virtualities into the practice of the everyday; it was television.

Nevertheless, what Wallace understood about television in the early 1990s, and what concerned him most, is not media specific, it was not unique to television. In fact, Wallace attributes the success of television and its deep integration into daily life to its ability to co-opt the metafictional techniques of postmodern literary fiction that were "once the best alternative to the appeal of low, over-easy, mass-marketed narrative" (173). Rather, what Wallace saw in television of the early 1990s was the generalization of metafiction's ironic mode as an orientation toward mediation. Given the degree to which everyday life is conducted via mediating devices of all kinds in today's wired culture, this ironic orientation could have seriously corrosive implications.

As Sutherland was inventing VR, Baer was developing the first console, and Pynchon was finishing *The Crying of Lot 49*, television was switching to an all-color broadcast. Unlike VR, videogames, and avant-garde fiction, TV's broadcast virtualities were already well-integrated into American life. By the 1990s, Wallace writes, "We simply couldn't imagine life without it" (167). With Americans viewing on average six hours of programing per day, television had become "something to be lived with instead of just looked at . . . as much a part of reality as Toyotas and gridlock." As television took on its prominent cultural role, Wallace notes, the United States underwent a shift whereby it came to see itself as an "atomized mass of self-conscious watchers and appearers" (161). Metafiction developed as an aesthetic form to reflect as well as engage in this mundane but centrally important cultural activity of watching: "If realism called it like it saw it, metafiction simply called it as it saw itself seeing itself see it." The realism function of metafiction thus depends on the expanded role of virtuality in daily life.

For early postmodern writers of the 1960s, this metafictional realism provided an important critical tool. Whereas television presented "versions of 'real life' made prettier, sweeter, better by succumbing to a product or temptation," self-reflexive irony could expose the disingenuousness, the inconsistency, the artificiality of the televised representations. Beyond its aesthetic value, irony seemed downright socially useful in its capacity for what counterculture critics call "a critical negation that would make it self-evident to everyone that the world is not what it seams" (183).[22] Even so, we should recognize in the structure of irony a manifestation of the ontological binary: the constructed, the seeming, the mediated contra the "real."

By the summer of 1974, according to Wallace, the effectiveness of irony's critical function started to wane. The Watergate scandal, which was mostly aired out on television, confronted audiences with "television's classic irony-function" (162). As the watching public asked itself, "If even the president lies to you, whom are you to trust to deliver the real?" television tried to fill the role of "the earnest, worried eye on the reality behind all images." All the while, everyone watching, even "a twelve-year-old," understood the irony that television itself could only offer more images.

Because television is "a bisensuous medium," what is seen on-screen and what is heard always threaten to contradict each other (161). Moreover, as discussed in the next chapter, the recorded image had already failed in its orthographic function in the aftermath of the JFK assassination. Even so, Wallace argues, the "credibility gap" made apparent during Watergate irrevocably altered the audience's relationship with television: "A nation was changed, as Audience." Television couldn't be trusted, and watching TV once and for all came to involve a guarded self-consciousness about the constructedness of its mediating representations.

Wallace calls what happened next "blackly fascinating to see" (173). Bisensuous television is "practically *made* for irony" and, following Watergate, it began "ingeniously absorbing, homogenizing, and re-presenting the very cynical postmodern aesthetic that was once the best alternative to the appeal of low, over-easy, mass-marketed narrative" (161, 173). Take as a contemporary example the way the NBC comedy series *30 Rock* handles product placement, with Tina Fey looking directly into the camera and asking Verizon if they can "have their money now."[23]

"The best TV," now for the last few decades, "has been about ironic self-reference like no previous species of postmodern art could have dreamed of" (159). Instead of attempting to cover over its ironies and project more complete fictional worlds, television began to flatter its audience for "seeing through" the projected images (180). Rather than promoting immersion, it

FIGURE 5.2. Tina Fey, in the *30 Rock* episode "Somebody to Love," makes eye contact with her viewers to make sure they are in on the joke.

encourages and even trains its audience to assume a self-aware ironic attitude toward it. To paraphrase Slavoj Žižek, TV viewers know very well that
what they are watching is constructed, biased, commercially motivated, and
artificial, and they enjoy watching anyway.[24]

Once TV has co-opted irony, it invalidates the established set of critical
tools. The "well-known critical litany about television's vapidity, shallowness,
and irrealism" starts to sound like the kind of bogus values against which
postmodern irony was originally deployed, and literary irony becomes in-
distinguishable from the aura to television it tries to critique (156). But what
truly bothers Wallace is that television trains viewers, for six hours a day, in
the cynical, postmodern ironic orientation. Inevitably, he suggest, our culture of watchers will take an ironic stance toward experiences other than
watching television: "'Television,' after all, literally means 'seeing far'; and
our 6 hrs. daily not only helps us feel up-close and personal at like the Pan
Am Games or Operation Desert Shield but, obversely, trains us to see real-
life personal up-close stuff the same way we relate to the distant and exotic,
as if separated from us by physics and glass, extant only as performance,
awaiting our cool review" (181). We can see here some resonances with a
mixed reality paradigm, though inverted. The watcher's ironic orientation
recognizes and acknowledges the paradoxical participation of the artificial
in her life experience, but does so in order to toss it out. Ontological distinctions drop away as the watcher receives all stimuli with the same ironic attitude; yet, rather than elevating the technologically dependent to the status of
reality, all experience instead becomes subject to a distrustful "cool review."
All reality is really ironic, artificial, constructed, disingenuous images instan-
tiated in media of all kinds.

Irony and Mixed Reality

The degree to which the ironic orientation has permeated U.S. culture and
the degree to which it can be blamed on television's successful training of a
viewing public, as Wallace suggests, are topics for another time. Regardless,
an ironic orientation is a devastating attitude for a wired culture in which
ever more of real social life is separated from us by physics and glass.

The version of irony Wallace saw in 1990s television promulgates wariness of all forms of mediation—technological and otherwise—in daily life,

regarding them as unreliable, potentially deceptive, less than real. It is the flipside of immersion (discussed in chapter 1), enforcing the same ontological binary that separates the artificially constructed from the relatively unmediated. Whereas the immersed foregoes critical self-awareness, suspending disbelief to explore the virtual, the ironic does not, rooting out and sneering at the false, illusory, or imaginary. The immersed at least allows herself, even if untenable in the long term, the indulgence of belief; the ironic, lest it get caught unawares, maintains the presumption of deception and disingenuousness. As a result, though today's digital communication technologies bring us the world at our fingertips, databases of text, image, and video on call anywhere with a few taps on a relatively affordable smartphone, the ironic orientation trusts none of it. All texts have biases and agendas, all images are potentially Photoshopped, all videos are framed, edited, and possibly staged. Scrolling alongside one another in a feed reader, Twitter timeline, or e-mail chain, reports of starving children in the Sudan appear to us just as "real" as the latest Internet meme or videogame trailer. They belong to the litany of media-generated virtualities on some screen, awaiting a "like," witty comment, or retweet.

Though Wallace speaks only about television, he does address the utopian discourses surrounding the coming age of networked communication technologies. Responding to George Gilder's predictions regarding "life after television," Wallace assumes an ironic mode himself: "Once all experience is finally reduced to marketable image, once the receiving user of user-friendly receivers can choose freely, Americanly, from an Americanly infinite variety of moving images hardly distinguishable from real-life images, and can then choose further just how he wishes to store, enhance, edit, recombine, and present those images to himself, in the privacy of his very own home and skull, TV's ironic, totalitarian grip on the American psychic cajoles will be broken!" (187). Going on, Wallace confirms that it is not the affordances of particular media that are at issue here, but rather an orientation that negates all mediations as inadequate and untrustworthy: "Jacking the number of choices and options up with better tech will remedy exactly nothing, so long as no sources of insight on comparative worth, no guides to why and how to choose among experiences, fantasies, beliefs, and predilections, are permitted serious consideration in U.S. culture. Insights and guides to human value used to be among literature's jobs, didn't they?" (189). Wallace recognizes that the real harm of the ironic mode is its capacity to dismiss irrealities and inconsistencies but offer no alternative. "Irony, entertaining as it is," Wallace writes, "serves an exclusively negative function. It's critical and destructive, a ground-clearing" (183). The proliferation of twenty-four-hour, on-demand, highly accessible information enabled by the Internet only exacerbates the problem.

Sincere Virtualities

In that last line, Wallace makes a dig at his fellow fiction writers. The self-reflexive techniques adopted from their "postmodern church fathers," now perverted in television's aura, feed an ironic orientation that offers only cynicism, doubt, and uncertainty (171). Wallace imagines the coming of a "new sincerity," a literary avant-garde that can espouse "single-entendre values" (193).[25] He finds himself unable to achieve his unironic aspirations, however, in even his own essay. After his sarcasm-laden critique of Gilder, he laments, "I am in the aura" (189). Three years later, Wallace would publish his masterwork *Infinite Jest*, a novel tormented by this same post-postmodern tension between irony and sincerity. However, even as he addresses the problem to his contemporary fiction writers, Wallace well knew that the stakes of this tension reach much further than the aesthetics of a new literary avant-garde.

Indeed, the question that underlies—and to some extent threatens to undo—Wallace's essay is how shall we regard these increasingly ubiquitous media-generated virtualities. Over the past fifty years they have become so integral to the everyday lives of our wired culture that we cannot imagine life without them. Our interactions with them have become so central to how we understand ourselves and our engagements with others that they are interwoven into what we have come to understand as realistic. And yet, over the same period, we have become well practiced in regarding mediation with distrust. Wallace focuses on the postmodern literary techniques emerging from 1960s and "youthful U.S. rebellion," which treated television's oversincerity and "bogus values" as a kind of spell to be broken, "the revelation of imprisonment yielded freedom" (182, 178, 183). We might just as easily point to the emergence and continued prominence of post-structuralist literary and critical theory, which has provided a vast toolbox for rooting out medi-ating factors of all kinds. In this context, sincere reception came to belong to passive, gullible, even complicit consumption, "the goal of a naive reader," as Jay Bolter puts it.[26] Taking a self-conscious, critical, deconstructive, ironic orientation toward these projections of culture, on the other hand, became not only intellectually and social responsible, but, as Wallace explains, hip.

Given the pervasiveness of mediating technologies in today's wired cul-ture, the persistence of such ontologically undermining orientations toward the virtualities of media have the potential to dismiss whole swaths of our mixed reality. But, furthermore, if we take this impulse to its logical ends, as Wallace suggests was happening in the 1990s, and assume this cool, ironic stance toward not just mass media projections but *all* occasions of media-tion in everyday life, we find we have little "reality" left to trust.

Such is the central problematic of Mark Z. Danielewksi's 2000 novel *House of Leaves*, and the subject of the next chapter. Hansen identifies *House of Leaves* as a novel for and about mixed reality, making it ideal for explor-ing literary fiction's place in the contemporary media ecology. But, following in the tradition of postmodern metafiction, it employs a preponderance of self-reflexive ironies, which have often led to charges that the book is ulti-mately nihilistic. I will instead demonstrate how the novel's articulation of Hutcheon's metafictional paradox challenges its readers to reexamine their own ironic orientation toward the text. In doing so, *House of Leaves* exempli-fies mixed realism and demonstrates its potential as an alternative to post-modern irony.

II EXTENDED STUDIES

6 When What's Real Doesn't Matter

House of Leaves

"This is not for you."[1] Johnny Truant's ominous anti-dedication and his first line in Mark Danielewski's *House of Leaves* initiates the warning that frames the text to come. According to the novel, Truant compiled the volume at hand from the notes of an independent researcher, Zampanò, who passed away before completing his authoritative academic study of Will Navidson's documentary film *The Navidson Record*. Upon discovering "reams and reams" of unorganized notes while exploring the deceased's apartment, Truant reports that he "sensed something horrifying in its proportions, its silence, its stillness" and for a moment felt "certain its resolute blackness was capable of anything, maybe even of slashing out, tearing up the floor, murdering Zampanò, murdering us, maybe even murdering you," the reader (xvii).

Zampanò had left "plenty of clues and warnings," even an explicit wish that readers would "choose to dismiss the enterprise out of hand," all of which Truant ignored as he produced the present volume (xix). Truant then spends his entire introduction warning the reader to set the book aside. "At least some of the horror I took away at four in the morning," Truant writes, "you now have before you, waiting for you a little like it waited for me that night, only without these few covering pages." But what threat could *House of Leaves*—a work of narrative fiction—pose to its readers, really?

Textualizing the Real Reader

In his analysis of readers who become subject to the fictional worlds of the text they are reading, Jon Thiem explicitly confines his area of study to the "textualization" of fictional characters, "that is, readers who are already characters in the fictional world of some text."[2] Yet, even as he makes this stipulation, he opens up intrigue into the possibility of "the textualization of real readers (if such a thing exists)." Despite Thiem's attempts to avoid the topic, the prospect of real readers getting "transported into the world of the text" haunts his essay. The mere possibility raises fundamental questions about the nature of the fictional: "What is the ontological basis, if any, of the fictional world? What is the fictional basis of the extratextual world? What is the reader's role in *constituting* both worlds?"[3]

The persistence of Thiem's wondering about the textualized reader speaks to just how tenuous the long-presumed boundary between fiction and reality really is. Wolfgang Iser, whom Thiem notes should not "be taken literally," explains that "'fiction' and 'reality' have always been classified as pure opposites," leading to much confusion and contestation.[4] Reading is itself a real activity, participated in by real people, interacting with real texts; however, the contents of fictional texts do not "denote a given reality."[5] Based on this seeming paradox, the act of reading fiction is often presumed to be divided between worlds of unequal ontological status: the actual world in which the reader reads on one side of the text, and the fictional world in which the events of the narrative transpire on the other.[6] Even so, though the characters, the setting, the plotline may not refer to actual entities, "reading is experienced as something which is happening—and happening is the hallmark of reality."[7]

According to Iser, then, if *House of Leaves* poses an actual threat to the real reader, it will manifest through the "happening" of really reading it. *House of Leaves*, indeed, seizes on the reader's real-world engagement with it and attempts to make the task of reading itself a site where the fiction plays out. The novel presents itself *as* a book, the second edition of Truant's recovery of Zampanò's study of *The Navidson Record*, and addresses its audience *as* readers. Similar to the videogames discussed in chapter 5, the real-world "happening" of reading the book belongs to the novel's fiction.

The fiction of *House of Leaves* has everted, seeping beyond the limits of its cover and pages and into the reader's lived environment. A prototypical transmedia narrative, its fiction spreads into notes, appendices, the copy-right page and cover, as well as several different editions—each with slight variations—a supplemental volume of letters by Truant's mother, a pop-music CD, and an online discussion forum, to say nothing of the variety of media objects it references or that have been generated and shared by the online fan community. This "networked novel" anticipates both being read and existing alongside innumerable other media sites, the central text merely "one 'medial presence' among others."[8] The novel's expressive manipulation of page layouts and typography anchor the story to the physical page while pushing the boundaries of what is possible in print even as publishing goes digital.[9] Its self-reflexive use of page space emphasizes the real-world, techno-textual exchange between reader and text. The resulting "reality affects" foreground the material act of reading, "experienced as something which is happening."[10] Instead of absorbing the reader into a fictional world, as Thiem fears, *House of Leaves* presents itself as already fully integrated into and par-ticipating in the reader's media-saturated reality. Hence Truant's warning.

Iser's discussion recalls Hutcheon's metafictional paradox addressed in the previous chapter. As I argued, the ontological tension arising from an "arti-fice" that invokes "intellectual and affective responses comparable in scope and intensity to those of [the reader's] life experience" has largely dissipated in the mixed reality of today's wired culture.[11] *House of Leaves* has consis-tently been read in this context, as print literature responding to its place in a digital media ecology.[12] Mark Hansen has argued that *House of Leaves* expresses "ontological indifference" between the compounding layers of media and mediation that instantiate its fiction.[13] For this reason, Hansen lauds Danielewski's book as exemplary of a literature for a mixed reality. As Hansen writes, "It is as if mediation has become so ubiquitous and inexora-ble in the world of the novel (which is, after all, our world too) that it simply *is* reality, *is* the bedrock upon which our investment and belief in the real can be built." For the reader of *House of Leaves*, however, this is a particularly precarious situation.

This chapter presents an extended study in mixed realism and consid-ers the threat *House of Leaves*, a work of fiction, poses to its real readers. The novel's expressive page layouts and technotextual self-reference fore-ground the materiality of the text, thereby negating any possibility of Thiem's immersive textualization. At the same time, these experimental techniques evert the perils of the fictional hallway they describe, transcoding them into corollary encounters with the text. The novel addresses the reader as "one 'medial presence' among others" within the "real" media ecology. The immediate task of reading itself invokes the reader's thoroughly mediated condition within today's wired culture. This mixed realism brings the consequences of ubiquitous and inexorable mediation to bear on engagements with the text. While the novel's demonstration of the failed orthographic function of media prompts a reinterpretation of the ontology of the virtual, it also raises the specter of a debilitating doubt and inescapable skepticism associated with a cynical postmodernism. Yet, rather than fall into nihilism, the novel's mixed realism challenges the reader to examine our responses to the fragmented, incomplete versions of reality on which we increasingly rely.

Everting Fiction

After a night of studying Zampanò's notes for *The Navidson Record*, Truant awoke to find he "didn't feel at all [himself]" and began to wonder for the

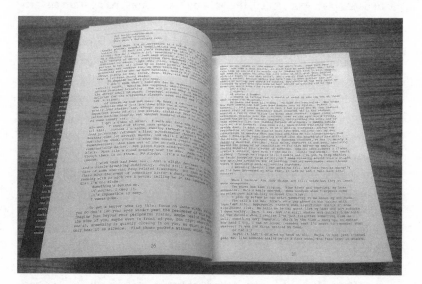

FIGURE 6.1. Truant instructs readers to "focus on these words, and whatever you do don't let your eyes wander past the perimeter of this page" in Mark Z. Danielewski's *House of Leaves*, 26–27.

first time if his reading had "actually affected [him]" (25n33). Still feeling out of sorts at work, he steps out into the hallway and has an overwhelming sense that "something's behind [him]" (26n33). Notably, Truant doesn't explain what happens or what he experiences. Instead, he directs his readers through an exercise premised on their physical orientation toward the book: "To get a better idea try this: focus on these words, and whatever you do don't let your eyes wander past the perimeter of this page. Now imagine just beyond your peripheral vision, maybe behind you, maybe to the side of you, maybe even in front of you, but right where you can't see it, something is quietly closing in on you, so quiet in fact you can only hear it as silence" (26n33). Rather than a description of Truant's panic attack, the reader's own feelings of foreboding take the place of exposition. Truant asks the reader to become conscious of the limits of her vision, to tune in to her proprioceptive awareness of the space around her: "Find those pockets without sound. That's where it is. Right at this moment. But don't look. Keep your eyes here" (27n33).

Electing to play along, I notice how little I can see beyond the edges of the page in front of me. I sense my own physical vulnerability while focused on reading: "Try to imagine how fast it will happen, how hard it is gonna hit you, how many times it will stab your jugular with its teeth or are they nails?" Something or someone really could be approaching from behind; I would never know until it's too late: "You should be running, you should at the very least be flinging up your arms—you sure as hell should be getting rid of this book."

This episode exemplifies the way *House of Leaves* transcodes fictional events and situations into a material experience of reading for its audience. Indeed, Truant's explicit goal in this passage is to give the reader a sense of what he experienced, not as he felt it but as an experience of reading the book. Foregrounding the materiality of the page and the act of reading ruins the possibility of immersive access to his specific experience.[14] Yet, at the same time, his demonstration incorporates the reader, everting the fiction into her immediate environment. The reader herself feels the threat, expressed via her own embodied orientation toward the text. Truant's demonstration, in other words, denies the reader access to the story in order to position her as subject to it.

Truant's explicit attempt to transcode his experience into a readerly experience offers a model for how to approach foregrounded textuality throughout the novel. *House of Leaves* frequently elicits embodied acts of reading though the manipulation of page layouts and typography. The effects of these manipulations go beyond description of narrative events to stage a separate, corollary experience of reading. Thus the signature textual deformations are not merely representational. They instead enact, as in make to really happen, the fiction for the reader.

For example, at one point during his final expedition, Navidson passes into a narrow corridor that gets smaller as he goes, and the text blocks describing his movement shrink from one page to the next. The first page on which he appears in the narrowing corridor the text is constrained to one inch of width in the center of the page. By the time the text box gets down to about five characters across and four rows down, Navidson is on all fours. The text box then flattens out to just two wider lines as Navidson moves from all fours to crawling on his belly. The size of the text box thus corresponds to the size of the opening through which Navidson can move. The use of white space conveys a sense of space in terms of print media, as the printed letters assume a concrete quality in conjunction with their semantic meaning. But, more than just depicting the shape of the hallway visually, the transforming text box affects the reader's own progress through these passages. As in Truant's panic attack, Danielewski forgoes describing Navidson's affective reaction to the hallway, letting the reader's affective experience of the page do the work.

Despite the relatively few words per page, reading progress—like Navidson's progress—is slow going. The standard page layout is designed for efficient and unobstructed movement through the text. Our eyes scan the tops of characters, along lines, and paragraphs, leading to the turning of pages. Left to right, top to bottom, verso to recto from front cover to back cover, the text block is the reader's module of transport not only through the fictional world but through the physical book as well. It is the medium of readerly mobility. Modulations in the shape of the text block produce corresponding changes in the reader's navigation of the page. The variations in line lengths lead to unexpected enjambments, slowing the reader's pace through this section. Sentences and words are broken multiple times, not only across lines

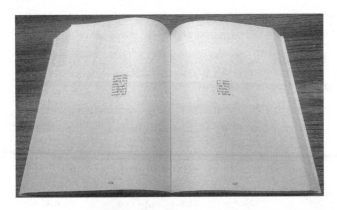

FIGURE 6.2. From pages 444–45 to 450–51 in Mark Z. Danielewski's *House of Leaves* the text box flattens from eight lines to two as Navidson must crawl to pass through a narrowing hallway.

but also between pages. While Navidson contorts his body to fit down the corridor, making sense of the experimental page layout slows the reader's passage through the text and requires its own acts of readerly contortion.

Of course, Navidson's predicament is much more physically demanding than reading about it. Having to navigate a two-line text block doesn't compare to crawling through a shrinking hallway. The experimental layout itself emphasizes the difference, drawing attention to the page and its defamiliarization of the reading process. It would be a stretch to call this even a metaphorical relationship. Instead, passages such as these foreground and emphasize the reading of the novel as its own meaningful event. The manipulation of the text block enacts a corresponding constriction in mobility through the passage as only a reader could experience. In this sense Navidson's traversal of the fictional hallway occurs for the reader as a "happening" of reading. The novel, it seems, doesn't contain this fiction; it is instead playing out across its pages.

House of Leaves consistently distinguishes, not only representationally, but also in practice, between the fictional events described in the text and the reader's task of reading about them. Its experimental layouts and self-referential passages cannot give the reader an embodied sense of what the characters are experiencing. They draw attention to the reader's meditated access and physical interaction with the text, emphasizing the difference between her embodied reading practice and Truant's panic attack or Navidson's experience of the hallway. Even so, the reading itself has stakes of its own, its own challenges, its own hazards. Over and above illustrating the circumstances of the characters within, the novel intends to demonstrate the reader's perilous predicament. To this end, it requires reading practices that correlate with the events and situations of its fiction, which enact problematics specific to the position of the reader.

Insides and In-ness Never Inside Out

One particularly prominent example occurs during "Exploration #4" as a blue-bordered text box containing note 144 cuts into the page. The box first appears on recto page 119, resembling an inset sidebar, slightly off-center to the upper right with the main text flowing around it. Turning the page to the verso, page 120, reveals another blue-boarded box, in the reversed position of the previous box as if framing the same hole. Rather than continue note 144, it displays the text from the previous page running backward as if printed on a pane of glass. Note 144 carries on like this—text appearing on recto, reversed on verso—until its conclusion on page 142.

Several critics have described the blue-bordered box as a textual window. Jessica Pressman, for example, suggests that as "readers maneuver" around these "windows" in the "physical wall" of the page "the novel blurs boundaries between the house on Ash Tree Lane and the house of paper leaves containing the story of this haunted house."[15] When these text boxes appear, however, the fictional inhabitants of the haunted house—Navidson and his expedition team—have just completed the three-day journey down the staircase into the mysterious hallway. Note 144 states explicitly that "there are no windows" (119). Hours into the fourth day, Holloway, the crew's leader, begins determinedly searching for "at least some kind of indication of an outsideness to that place." N. Katherine Hayles offers that the textual windows perhaps "compensate for the House's viewless interior."[16] But, of course, the reader is not *in* a windowless hallway herself. Compensating for the claustrophobia of the text is as easy as putting the book down and peering

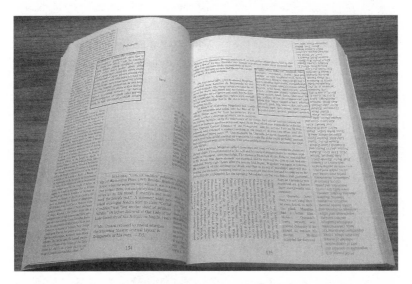

FIGURE 6.3. The blue-framed note 144 is surrounded by severe textual deformations in Mark Z. Danielewski's *House of Leaves*, 134–35.

out a "real" window. Attempting to look "through" these supposed textual windows proves much more difficult.

On the outside looking in, the reader might hope that these blue-framed panes, though they offer the expedition no view out, might offer a view *into* the hallway. They intrude at a crucial moment, as the crew confronts the endless "insides and in-ness never inside out" and fractures (119). Unable to cope with the cavernous hallway, Holloway abandons the group, shoots Wax in the shoulder, kills Jed, and disappears into the darkness never to be seen again, leaving the rest of group with little hope of returning to the surface. The reader likely expects the span of pages featuring the blue-framed boxes to offer some sense of their "desire for exteriority."

Zampanò, though, all but leaves the expedition. He provides sparse exposition of Holloway's argument with the group, his departure, and his gunshots. The events of the story are increasingly crowded out by citations of (fake) academic criticism about Navidson's documentary, the character of Holloway, or the shape of the house and an overabundance of notes offering categorical lists of tangentially related references, impinging from all angles. The blue-box pages are some the most chaotic in the book, though they do not much resemble passages in which characters explore the hallway. Moreover, after Holloway shoots Wax, on page 134, the expedition and narrative come to a standstill, even as the blue box continues for ten more pages. As Jed tends to Wax's wound, Zampanò transitions into a short essay on the waning indexical authority of film in the age of Photoshop.

In short, the blue-box section does not stage an expression of what it must have been like to be in the hallway with the expedition. Instead, it reflects and reflects on the reader's mediated position outside the text. The deformations of standard layout foreground the materiality of the printed page. A litany of citations and references emphasize and add to the layers of mediation between her and the characters. Narrative exposition gives way to a self-reflexive discussion of media and mediation. Looking through these windows, the reader sees only more text.

The contents of the box, note 144, reinforce her mediated, readerly access. Note 144 is an extensive list of common features of home interiors that do not appear in the hallway. No cooling or heating systems, no windows, not any sort of wiring, water pipes, or air vents, no lights of any kind, no communication systems, no moldings, no floor finishes, nothing made of wood (though the list doesn't specifically exclude ash), no insulation, no footings or foundation walls, no nails or screws, no interior indications of a roof or support structure. The only thing listed as present is the staircase the team descended. The note functions as a kind of inverse of Roland Barthes's reality effect, a "sample of reality" filtered item by item.[17] The excessive detail of Zampanò's list is eliminative, destructive of reference, working against a picturing of the house on Ash Tree Lane. Naming items not there preemptively eliminates elements the reader might supply from their own experience, a process key to imagining fictional places as habitable worlds. "~~Picture that. In your dreams~~," it concludes, striking the possibility of even dreaming an image of its construction (141n144).

Note 144 denies immersive access, preventing readers from conceiving the hallway as a real place outside their inevitably incomplete mental image. Yet, at the same time, by naming items not present, it still enters them into the virtual construction of the house, just under erasure like its gloating final sentence. Reading that a house does not contain a water heater, the reader likely thinks of a water heater then adjusts her concept of the house. Of course, this is not how anyone, fictional or otherwise, physically inhabits an actual room that lacks a water heater. It is, however, how fictional spaces described in literature are experienced: through the addition and subtraction of features, named and expected, until the reader has a mental image adequate to the purposes of the story. The exhaustive listing of possible features demonstrates how much detail is lacking from the descriptions of houses in a typical novel and how much the reader has to supply to flesh out the image. From this perspective, note 144 provides much more instruction regarding the mental construction of the hallway than it might seem.

The content of the blue-bordered boxes demonstrates in practice the difference between the experience of the house for the fictional characters and for the reader. The listed items do not exist for the house's inhabitants; Navidson never stops to consider why he doesn't find any "Arenberg, Chantilly, or Versailles parquet" (129n144). Those negated items are a part of only the linguistic construction of the hallway, part of the reader's reading of the narrative, part of the fiction. Enumerated under erasure, they negate the possibility of the house as they contribute to a mental image of it. The elements of a list of things not in the house have just as much reality for a reader as the house itself, all virtualities generated by language.

The blue box and its note 144 emphasize the fact that the reader's access to the described hallway is invariably and inevitably mediated by texts. The preponderance of notes introduced over the course of the blue-box pages reinforces this fact. Entering the text from unexpected angles, running for multiple pages, sometimes in reverse, these notes also foreground the printed page. Some even present a similar subtractive listing, like note 146, which takes up the left-hand, recto margin from page 120 to page 134 and names all the architectural styles not represented in the house.

Most of the other notes, though, take the inverse approach. They present exhaustive, digressive catalogs with no explanation of how they relate to the current circumstances. A few examples: note 147 (pp. 135–21), appearing backward and upside down in the margin, lists names related to any topic in construction; note 167 (p. 131), running sideways from the middle of the page into the spine, lists books and movies that could be said to "haunt" Navidson's film; note 182 (pp. 139–41) lists documentary filmmakers in two sideways columns read from bottom to top on subsequent rectos with the films they made in note 183 (pp. 140–44), forming similar sideways columns but printed backward as if in a mirror, on corresponding versos.

Rather than giving the reader a better perspective on the house, these notes multiply the original textual problem of how to understand the house when any understanding is mediated by language. They play the research game, compounding references in hopes that some constellation of the known provides insight into the unknown. Danielewski, here and through-out, anticipates the kind of relational reference that would be and will be prac-ticed in a scholarly analysis of *House of Leaves*. Not framed by an argument or editorial comment, these notes invite intrepid readers to look up all the entries in each list and draw connections. But that they appear this way, without explanation, suggests that Zampanò, the fictional researcher who compiled them, couldn't make much from a comprehensive comparative analysis and left the conclusions to his future readers. These notes thus pro-pose to send the reader down a rabbit hole of tangentially related texts.

Indeed, the individual entries in each note bear little obvious relationship to one another beyond a shared categorical heading. They perhaps better resemble the impersonal, algorithmic returns from an Internet search engine. An entered term—say, "documentarians"—sends back a list of links with the highest PageRank associations as determined by an esoteric machine analysis of a massive and expanding web of links between innumerable online texts. Each entry itself a potential search term, invoking another PageRank query, another web of texts. Thus these notes, hyperlink's print precursor, each constitute their own index of lexia. Search results listed flatly and without context, they await a Web 2.0 reader, whose pursuit of the hallway returns an ever-expanding database of texts in need of organization into a system of meaning.

Instead of facilitating access to the dramatic events of the narrative, the blue-box section of *House of Leaves* demonstrates how such access is constituted inescapably by a network of texts. In other words, as the fictional characters confront an apparently unending hallway, the reader contends with an unending archive of texts leading to more text. Yet this elaborate metaphor ultimately undoes its comparative function; the reader's mediated condition is fundamentally *not* like being lost in a cavernous hallway, as demonstrated by her inexorably mediated access to it. The blue-box section and its accompanying notes, instead, enact a mixed realism, coordinating the fictional with the reader's material interaction and circumstances.

Not coincidentally, the blue boxes appear on the "wall" of the physical page as Holloway kicks a hole in the wall of the hallway. His attempt "to find something, something different, something defining, or at least some kind of indication of an outsideness to that place," fails as the opening reveals "another hallway spawning yet another endless series of empty rooms and passageways, all with walls potentially hiding and thus hinting at a possible exterior, though invariably winding up as just another border to another interior" (119). For the reader, who comes to the hallway via the text, Holloway and his team's frustrated "desire for exteriority" manifests as an inability to get outside of language.

Looking "through" the blue boxes to find only more text recalls the old deconstructionist tenet that there is no outside, no fixed point to ground interpretation. The notes point away from the text with external references, but only to more texts. Invoking Internet-enabled research, they demonstrate that, in the information age, the inability to get outside the text has been exacerbated by the sheer quantity texts linked together. Like Holloway's improvised window that reveals more windowless hallways, these footnotes take us deeper into the abyss, leading only to more passages, with no guide, no windows, and no way out. Expressing frustration at these prospects, note 167 concludes, "To all of it, I have only one carefully devised response: Ptooey!" (135).

The point here, though, is not merely to be exasperating. Compared to the expedition's life-and-death struggle to survive the hallway, pointing out the reader's mediated access to fictional events is of little consequence. Yet, by running the reader through these occasionally annoying obstacles, the novel enacts and foregrounds the reader's mediated condition more generally, even away from the book at hand. In this sense, it constitutes mixed realism, as interactions with the fictional interact with the real. Here, the exaggerated task of reading *House of Leaves* exposes the reader to the stakes of ubiquitous mediation in a wired culture.

Between Two Frames

What is at stake for the reader in "Exploration #4"—and the novel as a whole for that matter—is the uncertainty and loss that unavoidably accompany mediated experiences. The sequence initiated with the blue-box section climaxes with Holloway shooting Jed in the face. Expressive layouts and self-reflexive prose articulate the stakes of mediation with the reader's own mediated access to Jed's death. In the process, these passages fold on to the task of reading larger sociopolitical questions about the increasingly prominent role played by inevitably incomplete media, particularly as it pertains to the formation of national identity and cultural memory.

So traumatic is Jed's death that it does not appear in the text at all. At the exact moment when Holloway's bullet meets Jed's upper lip, Zampanò's narration shifts—as it did in the middle of the blue-box section—away from the events in the hallway to engage with scholarly perspectives on the film. The transition reminds the reader that she was not reading direct exposition but a description of a scene in a documentary (and a second edition recovered from notes, at that), as it is displaced by a critical conversation about the futility of the "countless" frame-by-frame examinations (193).

Zampanò explains that "too many critics to name" conducted extensive analysis on these frames and were able to locate the exact moment of Jed's death in the time between frame 192, when the bullet strikes his upper lip, and frame 193, when it exits the back of his head. The film provides "ample information perhaps to track the trajectories of individual skull bits and blood droplets, determine destinations, even origins" (193). However, because the actual moment of death falls between frames, it crucially cannot offer "nearly enough information to actually ever reassemble the shatter."

Not only is the reader separated from the events of the story by compounding layers of mediation, the layers themselves are faulty and incomplete. The choice of "reassemble" here carries several meanings. First, it suggests that the mathematical calculations that could be used to describe the impact of the bullet do not add up to the actual happening. Moreover, in "reassemble" can be heard "resemble," indicating that the calculations are also inadequate as a representation of the event. Finally, they cannot "reassemble" Jed's shattered skull, so like Humpty Dumpty, all the king's men, mathematicians, film critics, and academics cannot put Jed back together again. Film analysis, discussion of the event, and even descriptions on the page are always inadequate, always tangential, and always too late.

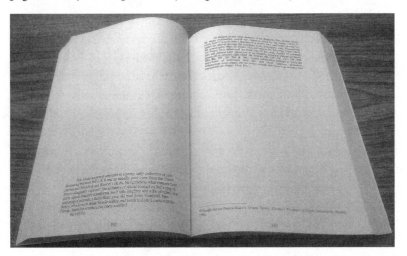

FIGURE 6.4. Jed Leeder dies between these two pages in Mark Z. Danielewski's *House of Leaves*, 192–93.

Here, again, the materiality of the page stages the circumstances of the fiction for the reader. In this case, the viewing of a (nonexistent) film gets transcoded into the task of reading the book. As Jed's death is recorded in *The Navidson Record* in frames 192 through 205, Zampanò's discussion of the recording in *House of Leaves* takes place from page 192 through 205, thereby indicating that the pages of the book correspond to the frames of the filmstrip. Tracking with the film frames, the moment of Jed's passing takes place between page 192, which leaves him hopeful that "he will live" now that Navidson has found him, and page 193, which describes the frame-by-frame analysis of his fatal gunshot wound. It thus falls between frames in print media as well. As the film fails to capture the moment of death, so, too, does the book.

The correspondence between fictional film and physical book continues from page 194 through page 205, with the unique layout of these pages emphasizing the discrete units of print media. As "chunks of occipital lobe and parietal bone spewn out in an instantly senseless pattern uselessly preserved in celluloid light (Reel 10; Frames 194, 195, 196, 197, 198, 199, 200, 201, 202, 203, 204, 205)," three sentences totaling thirty-four words are strewn over twelve pages as the trajectories of Jed's fatal head wound reach completion. The fragment concluding the text block on page 193, "Here then—," leads on to a trail of words from 194 to 205, that forms a single line, spaced with nearly a three-inch top margin, each page containing between one and five words: "Here then—[193] the after [194] math [195] of meaning. [196] A life [197] time [198] finished between [199] the space of [200] two frames. [201] The dark line where the [202] eye persists in seeing [203] something that was never there [204] To begin with." Broken up across multiple pages, these few sentences take a little more time to read. Their layout increases the frequency with which the reader must turn the page, which draws attention to the physical operation of page flipping and its mechanical resemblance to the passing of film frames between shutter and lens.

It is as if the frame rate of language has slowed down. For example, putting the two halves of "lifetime" on separate pages literally introduces time into a compound word. After reading "A life" on 197, the reader turns the page to discover she is still reading the same noun. "Time" announces its presence on 198 and the persistence of "a lifetime" across the two pages. The verb of the sentence, "finished," appears to bring "A life" "time" to an end on the next page, 199. However, it is not clear at what point exactly "finished" concludes "a life time." The actual moment of passing is represented neither in "life time," which denotes a living state, nor in "finished," which denotes a terminal state. Here again, even in summary, Jed's death falls between discrete units.

In this case, though, the "two frames" are not pages but words.[18] The sentences and words divided by substantial white space or page breaks draw attention to the fact that language itself is a patchwork of signifying units of varying sizes. Lev Manovich observes, "A human language is discrete on most scales: We speak in sentences; a sentence is made from words; a word consists of morphemes, and so on."[19] "Without discrete units," he notes, "there is no language" and, quoting from Roland Barthes, "language is, as it were, that which divides reality."[20] Jed's death scene demonstrates that side effect of this division is data loss. Slivers of reality slip irrecoverably between discrete samples, be they frames of a film or words leading from page to page.

Instead of narrating Jed's death, the text rejects the possibility of narration. The crucial moment is always in between. In light of this, Zampanò foregoes a description of the event as a combination of expressive page layout and self-reflexive language stage for the reader its inevitable in-betweenness. Jed's death scene, thereby, exemplifies Hansen's observation that *House of Leaves* subverts the orthographic function of media—specifically film and the written word—and replaces it with reality affects, an experience of the real "happening" of reading. At the same time, however, what concerns Zampanò in these passages is not primarily the failure of film to represent the scene, but rather how subsequent viewers, the "too many critics to name," respond to it.

The final sentence in Jed's death scene changes the focus from the discrete partitions of media to viewer perception. On page 204, "the eye persists in seeing" recalls "persistence of vision," the phenomenon of human perception by which a sequence of images shown in rapid succession look to be in motion. In this case, the persistent eye works to see *The Navidson Record*, as it does all film, as an uninterrupted, continuous recording. As the missing moment of Jed's passing attests, the recording is not continuous, but discrete. Still, rather than see the "dark line" for what it is, an empty interval between frames, "too many critics to name" persist in seeing Jed's death there (193). Their "frame by frame examination carried out countless times" proceeds from and maintains the illusion of continuity, that nothing has been lost.

Zampanò laments the endless calculations, analyses, and interpretations attempting to fill in that missing fraction of a second. It is not so much that they can never "reassemble the shatter," but their stubborn, irreverent reluctance to accept that Jed was irrevocably lost to oblivion in that absent instant. "Here then," Zampanò declares—in place of another "instantly senselessness" and "uselessly preserved" description of Jed's death—"the after / math / of meaning" (193–96). Splitting the compound word "aftermath" across two pages introduces ambivalence in the phrase. Punning on the calculations conducted to track bits of Jed's skull, Zampanò refers to the countless examinations and reexaminations, attempts to impose meaning between the two frames. All of this "after math" has come to stand in—here then—for the lost moment it can never recall. At the same time, the full compound, "aftermath," still resonates, implying ominously that consequences follow from the endless, futile meaning making. Thus, after acknowledging and conceding the failed orthographic function of Navidson's documentary and subsequent attempts at "reassembling" the lost moment, Zampanò adds an ambiguous sense of foreboding to this persistence in seeing "something that was never there to begin with" (193).

Here, as throughout, *House of Leaves* addresses the potential threat to the reader as well. Having established a correspondence between viewing the film and reading the book, the novel positions the reader to encounter and respond to the absent moment of Jed's death through the medium of print. Zampanò's "Here then—" points on to the text to come, a staging area for more after math and its aftermath. There, the reader peers into another set of dark lines, gutters between pages, an isolated string of text in black ink.[21] The text in this way extends a challenge to the reader, a test to see if she will join the "too many critics to name" by conducting a page-by-page or word-by-word examination in search of the missing moment and meaning.

Whether the reader can find anything meaningful in the absent half second of the death scene of a minor fictional character is of little consequence on its own. In fact, stretching the largely insignificant moment out for twelve pages might even seem fatuous and indulgent. Danielewski, however, invites

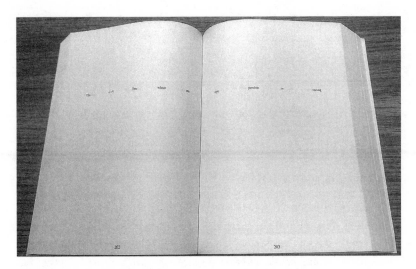

FIGURE 6.5. "The dark line where the eye persists in seeing" refers both to the space between frames of *The Navidson Record* and this line of text, in Mark Z. Danielewski's *House of Leaves*, 202–3.

us to extrapolate from this lost fictional moment the loss of real, historical moments.

Zampanò remarks that the volume of research done on Jed's death scene rivals that conducted on the Zapruder film, an amateur home movie that captured the assassination of John F. Kennedy. This passing reference establishes a comparison between the filmed deaths of the fictional character Jed and the real Kennedy. It points out that the 486 frames comprising the most analyzed amateur film ever similarly offer only failed attempts at reassembling what happened. In its orthographic capacity, the Zapruder film has become the cultural memory of a defining moment in U.S. history. However, as Jed's death scene demonstrates, the orthographic record is unavoidably incomplete, segmented by dark lines where the actual moment slipped between frames.

Kennedy, moreover, is emblematically linked to the rise of mediated culture. The winner of the first televised presidential debate escalated America's involvement in the first televised war (in Vietnam) and was notorious for allegedly gallivanting with a film starlet. Even after he died on film, the inconsistent memory of the Kennedy assassination has spun innumerable feature films and documentaries, television miniseries, and webpages in ceaseless devotion to the "after math." Joining the recording of his death here to Jed's calls into question cultural heritage writ large, the recordings, documents, and memories serving as bedrock for belief in reality.

The mixed realism of Jed's death scene, thereby, confronts readers with the inevitable gaps in all forms of media. It becomes an occasion to consider how we are to engage these partial records and the inadequate access they offer. Does one recognize the "space between" and acknowledge loss, or will "persistence of vision" fill them in and maintain the illusion of continuity?

A Viewless Interior

These questions take on a great deal of urgency in today's wired culture. Ubiquitous mediation truly is the bedrock of our belief in reality; but that doesn't mean it is any less incomplete, impartial, and subject to loss. "We live comfortably," Danielewski remarks an interview with Sinda Gregory and Larry McCaffery, "because we create these sacred domains in our head where we believe we have a specific history, a certain set of experiences."[22] But memory, even augmented by media, "never puts us in touch with anything directly; it's always interpretive, reductive, a complicated compression of information." He explains that his novel intends not only to inspire recognition of this aspect of our mediated condition, but to enact it as well: "In *House of Leaves* you're always encountering texts where some kind of intrusion's taking place. The reason? No one—repeat no one—is ever presented with the sacred truth, in books or in life."

This fairly reliable truth was of principal concern to literary postmodernists developing metafictional techniques in response to the cool images of television, as discussed in the previous chapter. A generation later, Danielewski borrows every one of those techniques—texts within texts within texts; historical figures in fictional scenarios; multi-media, multi-genre, and multi-sited narratives; narcissistic, sarcastic, contradictory self-referencing, et cetera—and blows them out to their logical extremes. By subverting the orthographic function of media and foregrounding the reader's subjective experience of the text, *House of Leaves* exacerbates the condition of which it is already a symptom. If mediation is the "bedrock" of reality but always an "interpretive, reductive, a complicated compression of information," then reality is up for grabs.

It is this realization that Truant hopes to spare his reader, dedicating to them his warning, "This is not for you." His is a tragic tale, itself an intrusion into the footnotes of Zampanò's study, of a life unraveled by the unexpected realization that "things are not how you perceived them to be at all" (xxii). Truant, our fellow reader, attributes his fall to his confrontation with Zampanò's notes, that "endless snarls of words" which sparked in him a deep-seated doubt capable of coursing outward from the text and into everyday life (xvii). "You'll detect slow and subtle shifts going on all around you, more importantly shifts in you" (xxii), as "a great complexity intrudes, tearing apart, piece by piece, all of your carefully conceived denials, whether deliberate or unconscious" (xxiii). When it has you, "then no matter where you are, in a crowded restaurant or on some desolate street or even in the comforts of your own home, you'll watch yourself dismantle every assurance you ever lived by" (xxiii).

This is how *House of Leaves* reaches beyond its few covering pages, not by thrashing out with beastly claws but by "grant[ing] you this awareness" of subtle shifts that can shake the bedrock of belief in reality (xxiii).

House of Leaves is a virtuoso performance in its denial of reliable truths as Danielewski negates or multiplies every entry into the text. To name just a few complications: Zampanò is blind so he cannot have seen the documentary he describes in detail; Truant is unreliable, blatantly acknowledges altering parts of his source material, and perhaps is insane by novel's end; none of the quoted sources can confirm Navidson even exists outside of Zampanò's notes; the house disappears after Navidson's last expedition; the videotape doesn't exist; a version of the text surfaced on the Internet before Truant had finished writing it; and Navidson burns a copy of *House of Leaves* page by page while in the hallway. There is even a suggestion that none of this ever happened and the whole novel was the invention of the clinically insane Pelfina, and that all the other characters, including her supposed son Johnny, are invented.[23] Pile on top of all these obfuscations and misdirections the multiplicity introduced by variations between editions, the diffusion of the narrative into multiple sites, the expansions and mutations that it undergoes in Internet forums and user-generated content, and the catalog of references the book invokes, and it becomes a veritable impossibility to settle even basic facts about what goes on in *House of Leaves*.[24]

By taking the voice of an academic study, presenting photographic and textual evidence, citing sources and triangulating references, the novel invokes real-world practices of meaning making. The shades of doubt that overshadow its fictional world are thereby cast in the real world as well, where similar networks of intertextual reference are relied on for veracity and authority. The novel seeks to expose a ubiquitous and inexorable uncertainty roiling beneath the surface of modern life.

Kicking a Hole in the Wall

The novel is for the readers of the text what the hallway was for its characters: transient, unstable, and, therefore, threatening. Stopping there, though, it would be easy to mistake *House of Leaves* for another example of cynical postmodern fiction, the kind David Foster Wallace would say is great at staging a coup but has no plan for governance. In "'This Is Not for You': Nihilism and the House That Jacques Built," Will Slocombe argues that *House of Leaves* "demonstrate[s] the absence upon which every presence is founded" but "it finally has nothing to say."[25] From this perspective, all the experiments with the layout, the labyrinth of texts, the metafictional techniques, the book's at-times smug self-consciousness seem like a bunch of tricks and language games.

And yet, fixating on what can and cannot be known is precisely the wrong response and, as Truant in particular exemplifies, potentially dangerous. Our fellow reader can offer no defense against the "transience of the world" the novel threatens to reveal, for he has none himself (23). The "darkness nothingness" he discovers while researching *The Navidson Record* leads to paranoia, delusions, and isolation (516). By novel's end, he is nowhere to be found.

House of Leaves might not have anything to say, thoroughly refusing, as it does, access to anything like a sacred truth. Instead, it has to be read for its mixed realism, for the way it makes the task of reading its fiction significant in the real world. Its play with layout and language confronts readers with their thoroughly mediated position, as enacted through engagement with the text itself, giving the immediate task of reading the novel weight and consequence within real-world contexts. While it may not offer up clear, unironic "single-entendre values," it presents readers with an opportunity to formulate a response, to reconsider the role of and their relationship to media and mediation.[26]

Touched by the World at Large

Just as it does for Navidson, this problematic comes to a head in the figure of Delial, the Sudanese girl in the foreground of Navidson's Pulitzer Prize–winning photograph. Zampanò explains that Navidson was drawn to photography because of his unstable childhood. Ignored by his parents, Navidson had been affected by "a discontinuous lifestyle marked by constant threats of abandonment and the lack of any emotional stability" (22). He took to photography as a way to isolate and preserve momentary certainties against the unknown and the fluctuating: "More than just snapping a few pictures and recording daily events with a few Hi 8s, Navidson wanted to use images to create an outpost set against the transience of the world" (23). So, when he meets Delial a moment before her death, Navidson tries to "slice her out of thin air" with a photograph. But, of course, as he relays to Karen in his final letter before entering the hallway for the last time, "that didn't keep her from dyding [sic]" (392).

Delial confronts Navidson with photography's impotence, its inability to establish stable outposts, as "not even ten thousand photographs can secure a world" (23). When Navidson found her, poor Delial was utterly beyond solution; he could not save her, could not rectify the global imbalances or Sudanese civil war that brought her to that position, nor could he make any claim to know her or understand her life and suffering. Her death demonstrates to him the inadequacy of photography and, by extension, any attempt to capture, settle, or preserve as a response to the inevitability of loss. There will always be death and loss and things we do not understand, and no photograph, no documentary, no academic research, no critical theory or work of literature, none of our "weapons (tools; reason)" can do anything to change that (37). Having suppressed this realization for years, Navidson acknowledges in his final letter his regret that she had to "go away like that," and that he photographed a dying girl rather than trying to comfort her or deliver her to her loved ones (392).[27]

And yet, though his photograph cannot still Delial's passing, the novel suggests it can serve another purpose. At Navidson's encouragement, Karen shoots her own short film in the house on Ash Tree Lane. At one point she turns the camera's attention to Navidson's photographs. Zampanò remarks the inclusion of Navidson's award-winning photojournalism "frequently permits the larger effects of the late 20th century to intrude" (367). One might note that the language of "intrusions" resonates with Danielewski's interview quoted above. Indeed, Karen's filming of her husband's photos proliferates her representation of him into multiple media sites and adds a few more layers of interpretation. But, at the same time, the photos expand the scope of the scene. Through this mundane occurrence, looking at photographs, "we are inadvertently touched by the world at large, where other individuals who have faced such terrible horrors, still manage to walk barefoot and burning from the grave." In other words, the appearance of Navidson's photographs in Karen's film is an instance of mixed realism.

The world intrudes on this sweet love story as it takes on a relationship to global poverty and the first world's mediated access to it. The only photograph given any specificity is the one depicting Delial. When Karen holds the Pulitzer-winning image to the camera, she discovers Delial's name written on the back, a name she knew only as the mysterious phrase Navidson had for years mumbled in his sleep. The function or effect of the photograph here is not to record, not to document, not to outpost the transience of the world. Instead it recontextualizes. Two distant circumstances overlap, impede on one another, a photograph the point of intrusion. Beyond questions of ontology or orthography, two seemingly unrelated milieus comingle in this mixed realism.

Whereas for the Navidsons this occurs through a documentary photograph, *House of Leaves*, here as throughout, everts to stage a similar intrusion for the reader in terms of her interactions with the book. Karen's discovery of Delial's name on the back of Navidson's photograph is accompanied by a note from the editors observing the image's resemblance to a real-life photograph by Kevin Carter, a photojournalist from South Africa who won the Pulitzer Prize in 1994 for his picture of a nameless Sudanese girl starving to death with a vulture looming just behind her.[28] Like Navidson, Carter was tormented by the image and received criticism for photographing rather than helping. Unlike Navidson, however, Carter could not survive her loss. Note 336 (p. 368) explains that Carter committed suicide less than a month after receiving his award.

The reference to Carter externalizes the narrative of *House of Leaves* in a way experimental textual variations could not achieve on their own, in effect removing the screen between the fictional story of the impossible shape-shifting hallway and the real world. *House of Leaves* may not textualize its readers in the manner Thiem has in mind, but it does position them in relation to the real-world problematics invoked by its fictional story. While it may be easy to dismiss much of the novel as nothing but fun language games, another work of contemporary fiction demonstrating its worth through increasingly esoteric navel-gazing, the Sudanese conflict and the global imbalances that produced the subject of Carter's photograph, the once-living analog to Delial, are very real. *House of Leaves* invokes those real circumstances and, in this expression of mixed realism, brings them to bear on the immediate task of reading.

For most of Danielewski's audience, the Sudan is photographs, news reports, and the occasional documentary. There is no record of the real-life Delial beside Carter's photograph, not even a name or a story of her fate following the snapshot. She is as real to us, then, as the fictional Delial, a virtuality of media. Print, photography, the Internet, and other media forms have given us access to anywhere on the globe. Quite literally, without the media ecology as it is, today's readers of *House of Leaves* may never have seen or known the real Delial. During the late 1990s, for example, Carter's photograph was featured in a chain e-mail, embedded alongside a prayer for the hungry.[29]

"Where do you want to go today?," Microsoft used to ask its customers. Our extensive digital communications technologies bring us the world; yet it is always and inevitably a mediated version, a "partial, incomplete compression of information." When an image of a starving Sudanese girl arrives unsolicited in one's inbox, all the careful critiques, like the essay on post-photography theory surrounding the blue-frame boxes of note 144, hardly matter. As Truant observes, "What's real or isn't doesn't really matter here. The consequences are the same" (xx).

House of Leaves takes on some of the consequence, and its capacity to do so is what I have been calling mixed realism. The novel activates a complex circuitry of interactions. The act of reading the novel, its foregrounded textuality transcoding its core conflicts into material experiences of reading, gets reframed by the fiction and becomes meaningful in numerous and distant real-world circumstances. All the little "intrusions" demonstrate the reader's thoroughly mediated condition within a wired culture, exemplified and enacted by the task of reading itself.

This recognition, of the ubiquity and inexorability of mediation in modern life, is a potentially dangerous one. Mediation still carries with it uncertainty, which *House of Leaves* threatens to spread beyond its covering pages into the media ecology at large. And yet the novel does not give into postmodern, nihilistic doubt. As Danielewski recommends in his interview with Sinda Gregory and Larry McCaffery, "We must be brave and accept how often we make decisions without knowing everything."[30] *House of Leaves* confronts its readers with an opportunity to do just that in response to the fictional Delial. As orthography fails and ontology blurs, it invites us to see connectivity, to think the exchanges between the fictional and the real, to recognize the relevance of reading to real-world circumstances, like global poverty. The next chapter will explore how mixed realism affords the opportunity to not only acknowledge but also potentially alter such circuitry.

7 Acceptable Losses

Call of Duty: Modern Warfare 2

A month prior to its release, Infinity Ward's *Call of Duty: Modern Warfare 2* (Activision, 2009) was already being discussed as a "terrorism simulator."[1] Footage of the game's controversial "No Russian" level, in which the playable character participates in a terrorist attack on a fictional Moscow airport, leaked on the Internet that October. *Modern Warfare 2* immediately reopened debates about violent videogames, a month before the game was even available to the general public to be played.

That a level in which players act out an armed assault on civilians at an airport inspired controversy is no surprise. What is interesting, however, is that the controversy about the potential dangers of playing the game can precede the possibility of playing it. It suggests the relationship a player can have to on-screen violence is somehow predetermined by the medium of interactive gaming.

A year later, this a priori critique was applied to the game again when a suicide bomber detonated explosives in the real Domodedovo Airport in Moscow. Despite the fact that the attack in "No Russian" is carried out with guns rather than improvised explosives, members of the media in the United States and Russia said the real-life attack "mirrored" *Modern Warfare 2*.[2] Further suggestions were made that these terrorists may have used the game to train, even though there was no evidence (that I could find) that the perpetrators ever played the game, which had been banned in Russia since its release. The irony of concerns about training with the game, of course, is that *Modern Warfare 2* descends from simulation technologies developed by the U.S. military for the express purpose of training soldiers. The extension of that fact here, regardless of evidence of any real relationship, demonstrates that the actual playing of the game has dropped out of these critiques. Anxiety over the threat of real-world violence posed by virtual violence remains strong enough to supersede the act of playing the game itself.

Given the videogame industry's track record, it is unlikely that a major-release commercial title like *Call of Duty* could handle such a delicate scenario like "No Russian" with sensitivity, nuance, or insight. In fact, the level's leak might very well have been a part of a cynical marketing strategy. For all the outrage the scene stirred up, within the first twenty-four hours of its release *Modern Warfare 2* sold 4.7 million copies in the United States and the U.K. alone. Demonstrating yet again the ambivalent acceptance of the military first-person shooter (FPS), these controversies seem to have done no damage to the game's sales figures. Furthermore, these conversations rarely have much to do with videogaming.[3]

Even so, that the critique can be and consistently is carried out prior to and without regard for the actual act in question—the playing of the game—has troubling implications for wired culture's thinking about media-generated virtuality. It suggests that the effect of playing, of interacting within virtual spaces, can be taken for granted.

We have encountered this thinking in the introduction as well, as California Deputy Attorney General Zackery Morazzini suggested in the U.S. Supreme Court case *Brown v. Electronic Merchants Association* that viewing video clips of gameplay would be sufficient to determine if playing a game would be detrimental to players.[4] The player's actual interaction with digital media, however, is considerably mundane compared to the "obscene levels of violence" on-screen.

The player has a controller with a set of buttons mapped to in-game behaviors that trigger responses from the console to render the on-screen environment, prompting the player for another button press, and so on. No matter how compelling a game world may be, the videogame player is not—as Chief Justice John Roberts suggested in *Brown*—doing the killing, the maiming, or anything equivalent to what happens on-screen. She is playing a videogame and her in-game activities do not have the value or consequence of actual violence. The hapless airline patrons who fall victim to the player's assault in "No Russian" are only the visual representations of an algorithmic process. Players can shoot them again and again and they feel no pain and they always return when the level restarts. Furthermore, the players know this and are metacognitively aware of this as a condition for play.[5] It is, therefore, remarkable that we show these inconsequential digital objects any sympathy at all.

Not only do a priori critiques of media virtualities obscure these increasingly common practices and their role in contemporary culture, they foreclose the possibility of different relationships to virtuality, of different articulations that might be forged within real social life. But how do we consider this realism?[6] How can we understand the significance of interacting with on-screen violence with an awareness of the banality of pressing buttons? How can we understand the gruesomeness of games like *Modern Warfare 2* as integrated into the lives of the players? In other words, what does "No Russian" look like from the perspective of mixed realism?

This chapter presents an extended mixed realism case study of *Modern Warfare 2*. It focuses on how the *Call of Duty: Modern Warfare* series uses the game's first-person perspective to organize a player's affective response to non-playable characters (NPCs) within the context of contemporary "virtuous" warfare. Military shooters like *Call of Duty* typically consist of eliminating wave after wave of interchangeable, insignificant NPCs. Though the prospect may outrage onlookers concerned about the apparent disregard for human life, players understand that these are infinitely respawning digital objects and therefore dispensable. The challenge for game makers is less often to convince players to overcome an aversion to on-screen violence as it is to get them to attribute worth, value, and significance to an arrangement of pixels.

Responding to this challenge, the *Modern Warfare* series uses its first-person viewpoint to personalize select NPCs by bringing them face to face with the player. Compared to "real" military encounters, however, such face-to-face confrontations fail to represent "authentic war experience."[7] When the U.S. military increasingly conducts its operations via real-time video feeds, networked surveillance data, and remote-controlled unmanned aerial vehicles (UAV), playing *Modern Warfare 2* most closely resembles *actual* modern warfare when it puts players behind the digital targeting interfaces of an AC-130 or the laptop controlling a Predator drone.

Many of the same concerns about desensitized digitally mediated violence extend to contemporary military policy.[8] As I will argue, the coincidence of affects toward the digital within the military-entertainment complex situates players of the *Modern Warfare* series in relation to the practice of actual war-at-a-distance. In this context, through their efforts to convince players to care about the NPCs they encounter face-to-face, these ultraviolent "terrorism simulators" become occasions for the articulation of new relationships to the virtualities of digital media.

This is not the first time a videogame has presented the opportunity for players to reflect on the relationship between gaming and militarized digital technology.[9] The *Modern Warfare* series distinguishes itself by situating gameplay in relation to modern military technologies through a full embrace of the conventions of the FPS genre. Ever since players squared off with cyborg Hitler in id Software's *Wolfenstein 3D* (Apogee, 1992), face-to-face confrontation with one's enemy has been a core element of the FPS experience. The *Modern Warfare* games are no different. Yet, in comparison to digitally mediated modern warfare, which is the subject material and context of the game, the spectacle of the face-to-face killing of another person has a quite different effect. As I will demonstrate, the *Modern Warfare* games in fact reconfigure virtual violence in and through the gruesomeness of confrontation itself. The game's first-person violence, even in the "No Russian" level, can therefore be a way for players to engage their position relative to actual modern warfare and the real violence mediated by digital technologies. In this way, *Modern Warfare 2* exemplifies how a videogame can operate as an "extension of one's own social life," with in-game virtualities taking on significance well beyond their often-violent content.[10]

Videogaming's Military Inheritance

The common practice when discussing videogames like the *Modern Warfare* series in relation to today's armed forces would be to collapse one system into the other on the basis of shared technology, shared ideology, or both. Ed Halter writes, "The video game industry from its very beginnings had never been fully discrete from the activities of military-sponsored computer research."[11] Given that much gaming technology was born from military-funded research and developed for military applications, and that many games, particularly military-themed games, express a pro-Western, shock-and-awe sensibility, it has become all but expected to read gaming as an expression of a military-entertainment complex preparing the next generation of soldiers.[12]

America's Army (U.S. Army, 2002) offers a perfect example to support this position. One of the most popular and widely distributed FPS multi-player games of all time, *America's Army* is both the product of collaboration between the U.S. Armed Forces and Microsoft and used to recruit and train new soldiers. These gamers turned soldiers find they are already familiar with the control interfaces of military technologies, after having logged hours in front of simulated versions in their favorite games. Moreover, following from Ronald Reagan's famous comment about the coordination of videogamers being ideal preparation for piloting jets, the military has increasingly attempted to cultivate this familiarity and facility, even using Xbox 360 and Nintendo Wii controllers to guide unmanned vehicles.[13]

With the use of remote combat operations, UAVs, bomb-defusing robots, tactical simulation software, and digitally mediated interfaces, many, including troops on the ground, have noted that war has come to resemble a videogame.[14] There is the feedback loop: videogames born from the military's need for digital technologies recruit gamers to operate those technologies. Games are an expression of war, which plays out like a game—in other words, the military-entertainment complex. So when John Arquilla and David Ronfeldt claim in a military report that the United States has an advantage in the war on terrorism "at the narrative and technological levels," it is hard not to see videogames like the *Modern Warfare* series sitting in the middle of that matrix.[15]

The simplest demonstration of the lineage of the *Modern Warfare* series is through the genre of the FPS. The first game to feature a first-person perspective for firing projectiles at combatants was Steve Colley's *Mazewar* (1974). Not only was it the first digital game to be played from the viewpoint of the protagonist, it was also the first online-multiplayer FPS, as it was distributed and played on the original ARPANET, which, by 1975, was under the control of the Defense Communications Agency. The first commercially available FPS was Atari's *Battlezone* (1980), in which players directed a tank through the perspective of its operator. The U.S. Army contracted Atari to make a military version of the game, *Army Battlezone*, that could simulate the operation of a Bradley tank. By 1990, *Battlezone*-style first-person tank training simulations had been networked as SIMNET, a dedicated multiplayer server for simultaneously training "hundreds of individual users at once, all operating in a real-time share environment, each representing any number of different vehicle types."[16] A military FPS with a robust multiplayer mode such as the *Modern Warfare* games clearly emerges from this coevolution and collaboration between the military and the videogame industry.

Around the time SIMNET was deployed, however, the nature of the relationship between the military and game developers changed. Budget cutbacks and new laws privatizing research and development coincided with the rise of videogaming as a commercially viable enterprise, altering the direction of each system's stake in virtual technologies. The simulations developed for military training had always "focused primarily on reproducing pinpoint fidelity to realistic situations" and, as a result, lacked "user-friendly engagement and 'playability.'"[17] "In a nutshell," Halter writes, "they were no fun."

By the early 1990s the gaming industry was developing its own technologies aimed to meet the specific demands of the entertainment market and amassed a catalog of "fun" military-themed games without direct military involvement. In fact, the rise of the videogame industry was due largely to the success of the Famicom home console—later named the Nintendo Entertainment System—manufactured by Nintendo, a company that famously refuses to accept military contracts.

This alteration of the military-entertainment relationship was responsible for the creation of one of the prime progenitors of *Modern Warfare 2*, *Marine Doom* (U.S. Marine Corps, 1996). A mod of the genre-defining *Doom*, *Marine Doom* replaced monsters with tan-suited soldiers and became what was essentially the first simulation intended to train foot soldiers.[18] Even though it was never actually used in that capacity, *Marine Doom* represents an important shift in the relationship between gaming and the military because it is an entertainment product ported for a military purpose rather than the other way around.

A Topographical Shift

In the years after, though the military continued to be involved in the development of select publicly available projects like *America's Army* or Pandemic's *Full Spectrum Warrior* (THQ, 2004), the simulation demands of the armed forces diverged from those of the entertainment market. The two realms continue to work together and share technologies, but the games produced for the general consumer tend to focus much more on fun and playability as well as cinematics and narrative. For military software, on the other hand, Ray Macedonia explains, "the object is not to entertain you, but to train you."[19] He continues, "I've been in a lot of flight simulators, and the thing is you realize, they're just like the plane. And if you don't know how to fly, you're going to crash it. So it's not an amusement ride."

The commercial release of *Full Spectrum Warrior* exemplifies the difference. *Full Spectrum Warrior* was developed to train U.S. Army soldiers in urban combat tactics. Instead of a first-person interface, users guide two squads, leapfrogging between buildings, as one squad lays down suppressive fire so the other can get into position. When the game was sold to consumers it included the military tactics trainer, but only as an unlockable mode. The main gameplay mode is clearly designed to be entertainment. It is much more forgiving and also has a fully realized overarching narrative, complete with individually characterized squad members.

The *Modern Warfare* series enters the military-gaming relationship here, as commercial entertainment media that makes reference to military operations. Like many other contemporary AAA, military-themed games, the *Modern Warfare* games do not re-create actual combat scenarios or practice actual urban warfare tactics; aside from hiring U.S. Navy consultants, they have no direct affiliation with the military.[20] One can easily trace the core technology back to military origins; however, given the independent growth of the gaming industry and the game's obvious investment in narrative-driven cinematic entertainment, it would be a mistake to simply assume that the *Modern Warfare* games are or can only be an expression of those origins. In fact, the *Modern Warfare* series incorporates this very anxiety about digital desensitization into its representation of the "reality" of modern, mediated warfare—and thereby, I will argue, opens the possibility for players to respond differently to on-screen violence.

Networks Fighting Networks

Infinity Ward's *Modern Warfare* series at time of writing consists of two games, *Call of Duty 4: Modern Warfare* (Infinity Ward, 2007) and *Call of Duty: Modern Warfare 2*, the first games in the *Call of Duty* franchise set in the contemporary period.[21] More than just updating the scenery and weaponry, the *Modern Warfare* series shows politico-military conflict to be in a state of transition to what Alexander Galloway and Eugene Thacker call the "fearful new symmetry of networks fighting networks."[22] During the opening credits of *Modern Warfare 2*, images and audio clips from key moments in *Call of Duty 4* are projected on a huge map as network nodes illuminate and streams of green light establish connections across the globe, indicating that the events of the first game expanded the network of influence for the second game.

Indeed, the events of the series narrative precipitate from the United States failing to recognize the limitations of opposing a networked enemy with a hierarchical force. In order to distract the world community while his Ultra-nationalists initiate the Second Civil War in Russia, Imran Zakhaev provides support for a coup led by Khaled Al-Asad in an unnamed Middle Eastern country. When the United States responds to the coup with thirty thousand soldiers, Al-Asad's insurgents detonate a nuclear warhead, wiping out the

FIGURE 7.1. The opening monologue and cutscene for Infinity Ward's *Call of Duty: Modern Warfare 2* present the events of the series as a global network.

U.S. forces. The remainder of *Call of Duty 4* follows the members of counterterrorism unit Task Force 141 as they uncover Al-Asad's connection to Zakhaev and eliminate the Russian revolutionary. *Modern Warfare 2* picks up five years later as Zakhaev's successor, Vladimir Makarov, frames the CIA for the terrorist attack on the Moscow airport depicted in "No Russian," instigating a full-scale war between Russia and the United States. Seeing this as an opportunity to get revenge for the thirty thousand troops he lost to the nuclear blast in the first game, Lieutenant General Shepherd attempts to destroy any evidence that would prove Makarov, and not the CIA, led the airport assault. Again, the remaining members of the 141 are the only ones who can prevent Shepherd from escalating the U.S.-Russian war and reveal the truth about what happened at the Moscow airport.

Even as Al-Asad's actions in the first game lead to open conflict of global superpowers, the outcome still depends on engagements between small, distributed, guerrilla forces such as the multinational 141, Russian, Middle Eastern, and South American insurgency groups, and contracted mercenaries. At the macro-level the series narrative certainly shows "nostalgia for the good old days of the Cold War," setting pro-Western U.S. and British forces against the rise of anti-Western, communist ultra-nationalism in Russia.[23] This showdown of global superpowers, however, is animated by an underlying network-versus-network conflict.

Faceless Enemies, Virtuous War

Videogaming's participation in what Galloway and Thacker call the "topological shift" of contemporary warfare has been well documented.[24] Exactly where commercial FPS fit in today's military-entertainment complex, however, requires more discussion. Significantly for our purposes, the military applications of those technologies common to the gaming industry aim largely at reducing or eliminating the kind of face-to-face altercation that is the hallmark and defining feature of the cinematic FPS. Galloway and Thacker explain that new technologies play a central role in the "emerging 'new symmetry'" of network-versus-network conflict. They remark that the variety of new formations like "information-based military conflict ('cyberwar') and nonmilitary activity ('hacktivism'), criminal and terrorist networks (one 'face' of the so-called netwar), civil society protest and demonstration movements (the other 'face' of netwar), and the military formations made possible by new information technologies (C4I operations [command, control, communications, computers, and intelligence])" are united by their common use of "new technologies at various levels."[25] This shift to network-versus-network topologies, buoyed by digital media, has the effect of *defacing* the opposition. Enmity typically takes an oppositional structure, allies facing enemies. When the opposition is a *network*, however, enmity is distributed and therefore has a "shapeless, amorphous, and faceless quality." A network is "a faceless foe, or a foe stripped of 'faciality' as such," and therefore the face-to-face confrontation of first-person perspective would seem ill fit to represent the structure of enmity of contemporary conflict.

Furthermore, the rise of this new topology is concurrent with the U.S. military imperative toward what James Der Derian calls "virtuous war." Similarly facilitated by the "technical capability" of today's military, the virtuous war attempts to minimize causalities to "actualize violence from a distance" by "using networked information and virtual technologies to bring 'there' here in near-real time and with near-verisimilitude."[26] Unmanned surveillance vehicles, satellite and real-time surveillance, and global positioning technologies support three-dimensional computer models, ballistics simulations, and long-distance precision-guided weaponry so that U.S. soldiers never have to come face-to-face with the enemy. The prominence of UAVs such as the Predator drone in current U.S. military strategy exemplifies today's digitally enabled war-at-a-distance. Predator pilots never need to see the battlefield with their own eyes, instead conducting their missions remotely via live feed of a camera mounted on the UAV. Using a network connection and control console to guide their drones, the Predator pilot engages enemies on the ground only as the pixelated silhouettes of his digital display. For this reason, the virtuous war is described frequently as "[reducing] war to a video game."[27] Thus a modern military videogame more closely resembles actual modern warfare simply by presenting players with digitally mediated violence than by representing first-person, face-to-face encounters with the enemy.

Gamer/Soldier

Both games in the *Modern Warfare* series are particularly aware of the role mediation plays in this kind of topology. In the first game, for example, players rush through a broadcasting station to interrupt Al-Asad's execution of President Yasir Al-Fulani. Players receive a bonus for destroying monitors displaying the transmission as they move through the station, only to find the studio empty. More than just including representations of media, the series frequently enlists the player's own television into its narrative, implying that home theater systems are themselves a site of modern warfare. Between missions, for example, as the player receives briefings, the screen displays satellite maps with marked objectives, building, vehicle, and weapons schematics, and personnel profiles, thereby casting the player's television as war room monitor. On other occasions, the player's monitor also fills the role of a civilian television. During the conclusion of *Call of Duty 4*, the screen displays news reports on the events of the plot. Then again in *Modern Warfare 2*, following the initial Russian invasion, the mission titled "Of Their Own Accord" opens with the vertical color bars of an emergency broadcast, instructing civilians where to find shelter. In this moment, the player is addressed not as a member of a ground troop or an elite special forces unit but as a television watcher.

These meta-media moments draw attention to the player's television screen by incorporating it into the narrative world, affirming the fact that we

FIGURE 7.2. The mission "Of Their Own Accord" in Infinity Ward's *Call of Duty: Modern Warfare 2* begins with this emergency broadcast, which positions the player as an endangered citizen media user.

are, in fact, safe at home and not engaged in military operations. At the same time, however, the game is unwilling to separate our engagement with the digital display and digitally enabled operations of the modern military. The player occupies a complicated position: one moment, a special task force agent, while the next, a civilian media consumer. This is not a military exercise; we are watching television, yet our monitors are implicated in the conduct of modern warfare.

Indeed, it is rare that players are equipped with a weapon that does not have some kind of digital interface, such as a red-dot, holographic, or thermal sights. Much of the game is played by looking at blips on the right-corner radar or a gun-mounted heartbeat sensor, which greatly augment the player's ability to orient herself in the 3D virtual space. The player's reliance on these interfaces becomes immediately apparent in the *Modern Warfare 2* mission "Second Sun" when a high-altitude nuclear explosion causes an electromagnetic pulse that knocks out all electronics and players must fight through the White House without the aid of digital augmentations. Modern warfare is presented as mixed reality, which suggests a relationship between the modern soldier and the videogamer established by their shared role as digital media users.

War-at-a-Distance

The concern about the co-articulation of gaming and war typically circulates around the disinterestedness of the digital. Both contexts share the same fear that repeated exposure to digital violence will train players and pilots to think killing is fun, war is a game, and the lives of enemy combatants are as dispensable as the thousands of digital representations gunned down onscreen, merely "a blip of logistics."[28] In fact, "because [drone] operators are based thousands of miles away from the battlefield, and undertake operations entirely through computer screens and remote audiofeed," the United Nations warns against the potential for operators to develop a "'Playstation' mentality to killing."[29]

The *Modern Warfare* series presents players with this experience as well, giving them access to simulations of laptop-guided UAVs and Predator drones and the targeting screens of attack choppers and AC-130s bombers. When players interact with these digital weapons systems, the vantage leaves

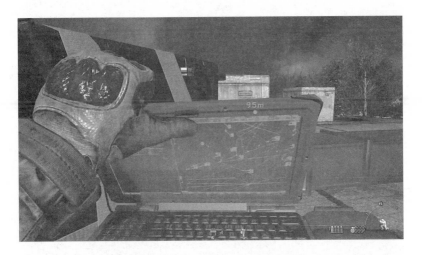

FIGURE 7.3. To fire a Predator missile in Infinity Ward's *Call of Duty: Modern Warfare* 2, the player's character opens a laptop. The player's screen is then overtaken with a targeting interface, displaying the perspective of the unmanned aerial vehicle from which the missile will launch.

the standard FPS perspective, which is always embodied in an avatar's hands gripping a trigger, and fills the screen with the accurate representation of the real targeting display. Rather than showing the avatar's fingers pushing buttons on a console or the interior of the aircraft that would be in the gunner's peripheral view, the player's monitor itself simply becomes the targeting interface and his controller, the trigger. Whereas the player's mediated position undermines the first-person experience of ground combat, it reinforces his role as a remote combat specialist because both gamer and pilot are digital media users. Both sit in front of a monitor, miles from any actual fighting, use a computerized control interface to fire on a distant battlefield they will never physically inhabit, and are therefore susceptible to a "'Playstation' mentality." Of course, when the player pulls his trigger, no actual bomb is deployed.

In addition to the replication of realistic interfaces, *Modern Warfare* series also simulates radio chatter on the AC-130 ship. Chatter is most prominent in *Call of Duty 4*'s "Death from Above" level, in which players act as the ship's gunner throughout the entire mission. The structure of the mission is relatively simple: the AC-130 has been called in to provide air support for a team on the ground that is attempting to move a VIP to a landing zone to be

FIGURE 7.4. The gunman's targeting interface on the AC-130 during the "Death from Above" mission in Infinity Ward's *Call of Duty 4: Modern Warfare*.

extracted by a helicopter. The player's goal is to protect the team, marked with flashing beacons, from having to engage hostile personnel face-to-face. As the player proceeds to clear the map of unblinkered silhouettes, the voices of several team members give tactical information and instruction regarding the status of the ground team, the movements of friendly vehicles, the readiness of various weapons, and the location of enemy personnel and ambush points.

Alongside the mission data, these disembodied voices provide feedback regarding the success of the player's shots. Hits are footnoted with comments such as "Hot damn!" or "Woah!"—suggesting awe at the explosive spectacle—or, more chillingly, understated confirmations such as "Yup, that was right on target," "Roger, you got that guy. Might have been within two feet of him," "Yeah, good kill. I see lots of little pieces down there," or, just simply, "Ka-boom." The majority of the game is fought as a soldier on the ground and is thus characterized by a chaotic barrage of escalating gunfire and explosions. High above the battlefield, by contrast, combat is eerily serene. The AC-130 gunner hears only the radio chatter, the sound of the plane engine, and the deployment of weapons, but not their collision with the earth. The detachment from the line of fire is reflected in the radio chatter's detached attitude toward the loss of human life on the ground below.

The "Death from Above" mission concludes with one of the squad members commenting, "This is going to be one hell of a highlight reel." Though it can be taken as a metaphor describing a successful operation, this comment could also refer to a tape recording of the mission. The U.S. military records many of its bombings for both evaluation and training. These "highlight reels" also circulate in unofficial capacities on the Internet in celebration of successful missions and martial prowess.[30] Referred to as "war porn," these videos frequently include playback of radio chatter, which sound much like the headset-enabled chat of online multiplayer sessions and are characterized by the same impassivity as that replicated in *Call of Duty 4*.[31] The realistic representation of *Call of Duty 4* encompasses the appearance and behavior of real weapons as well as the affect of digitally mediated warfare.

The ambivalence of the simulated radio chatter in the "Death from Above" mission situates the gamer in relation to military technologies as well as the political and ethical implications of their use. The mission makes explicit

the connection between videogaming and remote combat through a fundamental problematic applicable to both media: the possibility that the ephem-
erality of on-screen displays desensitizes users to violence done to real human
beings. Of course, representations of digital mediation never draw the protests of parent groups and politicians. *Call of Duty 4* certainly has a sufficient
level of gore to warrant its "Mature" rating. Yet the haunting indifference of
the radio chatter in "Death from Above" is infinitely more disquieting than
the stylized and innumerably repeated death animations that litter the screen
throughout the majority of the game.

   The reason, I argue, is this articulation of simulated and real digitally
mediated warfare. For all the high-definition graphics and advanced interactive technology, videogaming's "obscene" depictions of violence never quite
come off as realistic, for they are always belied by the player's embodied
position, holding a plastic controller while sitting in front of a monitor. In
the "Death from Above" sequence, that disassociation breaks down as players confront their position in a military-entertainment complex. Unlike the
fantastic first-person gunfights on the ground, the actual playing of which
is nothing remotely close to the experience of what it represents, when players fire bombs from behind the simulated targeting system they engage the
very technology, logics, and affect of the virtuous war.

   Contrary to a long literary tradition describing "authentic war experience"
as the brutality of killing another person face-to-face, Slavoj Žižek points out
that in contemporary conflicts technology typically mediates engagement
with opposing forces. "The truly traumatic feature [of combat]," therefore,
"is *not* the awareness that I am killing another human being (to be obliter-
ated through the 'dehumanization' and 'objectivization' of war into a technical procedure) but, on the contrary, this very 'objectivization,' which then
generates the need to supplement it by fantasies of authentic personal encounters with the enemy."[32] It is precisely this inversion that players experience in "Death from Above," removed from the graphic and deadly first-person
gun battle to drop bombs on digital silhouettes, accompanied by the dispassionate applause of radio chatter. Disquiet comes with the recognition that
"it is thus not the fantasy of a purely aseptic war run as a videogame behind
computer screens that protects us from the reality of the face to face killing
of another person; on the contrary it is this fantasy of face to face encounter

with an enemy killed bloodily that we construct in order to escape the Real of the depersonalized war turned into an anonymous technological operation." From this perspective the "obscene" level of high-definition gore in contemporary games obscures the reality of technologically efficient modern warfare. At the same time, however, the unease that accompanies our confrontation with that reality in the ambivalence of the radio chatter suggests the potential for a different relationship to the objectivized digital silhouettes. The radio chatter validating and encouraging the elimination of the remediated soldiers paradoxically confers on those insignificant virtualities a degree of humanity when the player recognizes in them the real-life victims of digitally mediated war to which they are iconically linked. Even though these NPCs bear no connection to any specific real person and are merely the graphic display of an algorithmic process, they invoke the problematics of modern warfare in a way that opens the possibility for players to respond to the digital in new ways.

Face to Face

Žižek's point is on display throughout the *Modern Warfare* series, but explicitly as the game repeatedly recasts the "technical operation" of button pushing as the "authentic war experience" of face-to-face confrontation. In the most dramatic examples of this technique, the playable character is shot or maimed straight on from close range with the first-person camera positioned to look the enemy in the eye. During the opening credits of *Call of Duty 4*, for example, the player takes limited control of President Al-Fulani as Al-Asad executes him with a gunshot to the face.

The cinematic structure of this scene is repeated multiple times in the second game, notably in betrayals by Makarov and Shepherd. Both games also conclude with similar face-to-face confrontations, but with the player's character issuing the final blow. In both games, but particularly in *Modern Warfare 2*, the final "boss battle" stands in stark contrast to the spectacular pyrotechnics leading up to that moment. After a fantastic high-speed boat chase during which Captain Price shoots down Shepherd's get-away helicopter before going over a waterfall, *Modern Warfare 2* concludes with a bloody fistfight. The playable character, Soap MacTavish, is disarmed of his knife by Shepherd, who plunges his own blade into Soap's chest. Shepherd draws

FIGURE 7.5. In Infinity Ward's *Call of Duty 4: Modern Warfare* the player witnesses the filmed assassination of President Yasir Al-Fulani from the first-person perspective.

his revolver and aims it into the viewport for another face-to-face execution. Just before he pulls the trigger, Price returns and knocks the gun away. The player and the mortally wounded Soap can only watch as Price exchanges punches with Shepherd just beyond the hilt of the protruding knife. Shepherd eventually gets the better of Price and begins pounding him repeatedly. The player, through furious button mashing, directs Soap to pull the knife from his own chest and, with a pull of the gamepad trigger, lodge it between Shepherd's eyes. *Modern Warfare 2*, a game played largely through the remediated interfaces of radars, heartbeat sensors, and remote targeting systems, thus concludes with gruesomely analog combat.

By using first-person perspective to place players in face-to-face confrontations with enemy NPCs, the *Modern Warfare* series adds a visceral brutality to these virtual, immaterial altercations. The drawn-out, cinematic viciousness of these close-range conflicts also marks them off from the numberless NPCs encountered over the course of the game. The first-person standoffs with major enemies—Al-Asad, Makarov, Zakhaev, and General Shepherd—grant these characters individuality and importance over the hundreds of their nameless soldiers the player dispatches to get to them. Moreover, putting the player face-to-face with her executioner or betrayer reconstitutes

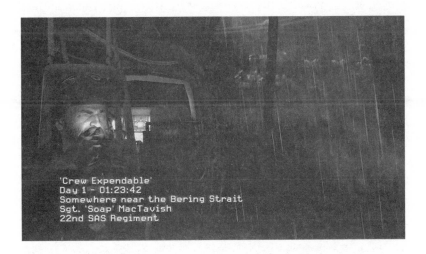

'Crew Expendable'
Day 1 - 01:23:42
Somewhere near the Bering Strait
Sgt. 'Soap' MacTavish
22nd SAS Regiment

FIGURE 7.6. The face-to-face introduction of Captain Price in Infinity Ward's *Call of Duty 4: Modern Warfare* is echoed in Infinity Ward's *Call of Duty: Modern Warfare* 2 for the introduction of Soap MacTavish, the playable character from the first game who has become Price's replacement.

the game's underlying network-versus-network conflict as a one-on-one showdown. Set aside global, multilateral antagonisms, when Al-Asad looks the player straight in the eye before pulling the trigger his becomes the face of enmity and the fight is made personal. The face-to-face confrontation, therefore, plays a key role in organizing the plot, justifying the player's actions against countless NPC baddies, and establishing the emotional structure of the game experience.

In addition to personalizing enmity, face-to-face interactions personalize friendly NPCs as well. Take for example the opening sequence of the first non-tutorial mission of *Call of Duty 4*, "Crew Expendable," shot opposite Captain Price, professional badass, calmly smoking a cigar before boarding an enemy boat from a helicopter. This scene is echoed in *Modern Warfare 2* as the player watches Soap, the main playable character from the first game, finish his own cigar. This shot establishes Soap as Price's replacement and the player's commanding officer, demonstrates Soap's admiration for his predecessor, and sets the stage for their reunion later in the game.

Aside from the lengthy between-level monologues by Shepherd and Price, there is little conversation to define personalities or relationships. Moreover, the player is constantly shifting between avatars and locations. With few

FIGURE 7.7. The previously unknown Private Wade hands the player a gun before being shot in Infinity Ward's *Call of Duty: Modern Warfare 2*.

characters speaking more than a couple lines or phrases and the frequent shifts in narrative context, these face-to-face presentations can quickly clarify who is who and how they relate to the playable character. Whereas face-to-face betrayals characterize the few significant enemies, teammates and friends rescue the player's character or pull him up from the ground. Saving the player from a brutal first-person death builds a sense of camaraderie and trust, presenting the NPC to the player as someone about whom to care. This method can work almost instantaneously, as at the beginning of the mission "Second Sun" in Modern Warfare 2 when a previously unknown NPC hands the player a gun and is immediately shot in the head.

Even Shepherd first appears on-screen to pick up the playable character Joseph Allen. The game thus introduces him as a trustworthy compatriot, setting up his betrayal later in the narrative. Shepherd's face-to-face betrayal, in fact, comes just after a face-to-face rescue by 141 squad mate Ghost. At the conclusion of the "Loose Ends" mission, the player's character, Roach, falls while trying to escape Makarov's compound. Ghost drags and then supports him the rest of the way to the extraction point. Just as it seems they are in the clear with their commanding officer, Shepherd, coming to congratulate them, Shepard immediately shoots both Roach and Ghost at point-blank range. The impact of Shepherd's betrayal in this scene is amplified because it follows after Ghost's rescue moments earlier, which had reinforced his importance to the playable character right before both are killed.

While this technique typically serves a narrative purpose—establishing relationships, heightening suspense, and so forth—it can also introduce the possibility for players to respond to digital characters with greater deference. The first-person perspective in the Modern Warfare series attaches emotional significance to the non-playable characters through the visceral quality of the face-to-face encounter, setting up players to have an affective reaction to the fate of an arrangement of pixels. A striking example occurs in a seemingly meaningless sequence of events during the final mission of the game. On the trail of Shepherd, Price and Soap must get past his private army of mercenaries to infiltrate his secret hideout. Much of the assault is typical of the rest of the game, involving stealthy movements and silent takedowns. One interaction, however, has a unique animation that sets it apart from the rest of the game. Price and Soap use cables to descend a cliff face and come down

FIGURE 7.8. The player first meets Colonel Shepherd as he helps the playable character Allen to his feet in Infinity Ward's *Call of Duty: Modern Warfare 2*. Eventually Shepherd will betray the player face-to-face, executing Ghost and the playable Roach from close range. He then sets fire to their bodies with a lit cigar.

directly on top of two unsuspecting guards. Playing as Soap, hanging above his prey, the player presses a button that initiates a cutscene in which Soap drops down on one of the guards, stabs him in the chest, and muffles his mouth so he cannot alert other mercenaries. The camera's first-person perspective on this silent takedown puts the player face-to-face with his victim, looking into the eyes of the dying guard as they roll back in his head and his body goes limp.

This sequence appears to be an almost literal example of Žižek's comment. The player's banal pull of a trigger, one of thousands performed in the game, initiates a series of mathematical processes with ties to the depersonalizing technologies that enable war-at-a-distance, depicted visually as the vicious "face to face killing of another person." Yet, despite the verisimilitude of next-generation HD graphics, the player knows very well that this is not another person. For Žižek, the "fantasy of face to face encounter" is constructed to retain some sense of humanity for the fallen soldier who "has his death, like his life, managed by a computer in a blip of logistics."[33] Here, however, we have just the computer blip, just the mathematical process, to be executed without remorse or consequence. No life, only code. This scene, therefore, cannot be read, as Žižek would have it, as constructed "to escape

FIGURE 7.9. Knifed in the chest, this non-playable character looks the player in the eye as he dies in Infinity Ward's *Call of Duty: Modern Warfare 2*.

the Real of the depersonalized war," because it asks players to conduct the humanizingly brutal kill by means of what is *already* an "anonymous technological operation." Making eye contact with this algorithm, in effect, counteracts this technological anonymity by challenging the player to see a human face in the digital display.

The player is presented with this problematic again in the very next sequence. Immediately after the gruesome face-to-face cutscene, Price and Soap move into the cave serving as Shepherd's base. Just inside they come upon a single soldier with his back to the cave entrance, smoking and watching a monitor. Price instructs the player not to engage the target as the two slip into the shadows to avoid a passing patrol, which leaves the lone mercenary with his television. Price then gives the player the option to kill this hapless guard or let him to exit the room on his own. This scenario has the same basic setup as the player's previous encounter: an unsuspecting guard standing between the player and his objective. The difference is that in the previous encounter the player had no choice about how to proceed. Dangling from a rope over two guards, the player had no other option but to pull the trigger and initiate a gruesome cutscene. Here we remain in-engine, retaining

Price: Take out the guard having a smoke, or wait for him to move along.

FIGURE 7.10. After the face-to-face knifing of a guard in the previous sequence of Infinity Ward's *Call of Duty: Modern Warfare 2* (see figure 7.9), the player's next opportunity to eliminate an enemy is presented as a choice: "Take out the guard having a smoke, or wait for him to move along."

interactivity, and are given the choice, just after initiating the face-to-face killing of another person, to kill again or not.

One might expect, given the popularity of morality mechanics in contemporary major-release videogames, that this choice would have some narrative or gamic consequence.[34] On the level of gameplay, however, the player's decision here makes no difference, and consideration for the life or death of the NPC never enters the equation. Under the logic of the player's mission objectives, the determination to kill or wait is decided by efficiency; this is a low-level objective standing between the player and the high-level objective. Regardless of how the player deals with the smoking guard, the choice affects only the number of guards that engage him directly before he exits the room. The decision to kill or wait thus has the same significance as selecting a weapon: merely a matter of playstyle. The introduction of choice, however, intervenes in the overriding logic of efficiency. Following the harrowing face-to-face encounter of the previous sequence, the option to kill or wait presents an opportunity to enact the game mechanics through a more humanizing perspective. Regardless of whether players decide to shoot the TV-watching guard, they might recognize in the arrangement of pixels a life worth sparing—even if this inconsequential, infinitely respawning NPC is not.

Sympathy for NPCs

Offering players the opportunity to reevaluate their relationship with the digital in the context of modern warfare is ultimately the achievement of the controversial "No Russian" level as well. For "No Russian," the game's narrative explicitly frames the player's participation within the objectivized logic of war. In order to keep tabs on Makarov, Shepherd handpicks the playable character Joseph Allen to infiltrate the inner circle of Makarov's terror cell. During the between-mission briefing, Shepherd explains to Allen the cost-benefit analysis of maintaining his cover no matter what: "You don't want to know what it's cost to put you next to him. It will cost you a piece of yourself. It will cost nothing compared to everything you'll save." From the outset, then, the mission is justified through a utilitarian calculation; whatever unspeakable things Allen must do to gain Makarov's trust will be warranted by the lives saved in the end. The scene opens with Allen in an elevator with several heavily armed men in suits. One of the men, Makarov, seen by the player for the first time face-to-face, turns back to the camera as he says calmly, "Remember, no Russian." The doors of the elevator open as the armed men walk slowly out into the terminal and open fire on the civilians standing in line for their flights. The shooting begins without warning or explanation. Running and sprinting are disabled, forcing the player to walk slowly through the slaughter. The player may shoot the unarmed civilians or not—the level still creeps slowly forward regardless. Firing on Makarov's team restarts the mission. NPCs run ahead trying to escape, some are injured dragging themselves to safety, a few attempt to help their downed compatriots. The corridor is full of bodies, blood, and baggage as the automated departures board flips all flights to "cancelled."

There is nothing fun about this level. It is shocking and uncomfortable, and it is hard to know what to do or how to feel the first time through. Part of that is the fault of the game. The narrative of *Modern Warfare 2* can be obtuse, hard to follow, and often illogical. Tom Bissell calls the "No Russian" scene in particular "morally confused and dramatically lazy."[35] Despite its flaws, the scene is not, as Bissell concludes, "a kind of pointless test," precisely because of how the game positions players as digital media users within a military-entertainment complex. The "test" of "No Russian" is not how one would

FIGURE 7.11. The victims of Makarov's airport assault turn to face the player in Infinity Ward's *Call of Duty: Modern Warfare 2*.

react if one were in Allen's shoes. That decision has already been scripted into the narrative: Allen chooses to let the massacre happen, sacrificing the few for the many Shepherd told him were at stake. The test for the player, rather, is whether he can recognize in these arrangements of pixels enough humanity to care about what happens to virtual victims. By putting players face-to-face with helpless targets, "No Russian" is structured to evoke an affective response to utterly inconsequential NPCs that are no more and no less than digital objects. Not only are these digital victims literally numerical values, Shepherd's voiceover framing the missions values them numerically. These are acceptable losses in a global conflict. Even so, players will likely feel some degree of sympathy for these virtual victims and have concerns about their own involvement in what happens to them.

While this may not seem like much on its own, in the context in which the game was released it is extremely significant. As the media debated *Modern Warfare 2*, "the terrorism simulator," the CIA escalated its use of Predator drone strikes in Pakistan.[36] The same month that footage of "No Russian" leaked, it was reported that three years of bombing had caused an estimated 320 civilian casualties.[37] Over the next year, the number of strikes more than doubled, confirming that remote, digitally mediated attacks had become a central strategy in the war on terror.[38] When viewed in this context, instead of through concern about the potential effects of violent videogames, the "No Russian" sequence looks quite different. Rather than training players to be unaffected by (digital representations of) violence, the level is purposefully staged to affect and *resensitize* players and their interaction with the virtual. With run and sprint disabled, players must linger in the carnage of "No Russian" and watch it unfold. Even though the virtual airport patrons are utterly dispensable, just a visual display of a string of numbers that spring back to life immediately when one reboots the game, seeing them die is uncomfortable and disconcerting—and it is supposed to be. "No Russian" succeeds by raising questions about how one is to "play" such a gruesome level as well as about the justified costs of war now frequently conducted through "a blip of logistics." By responding with sympathy for defenseless human beings represented by digital graphics, players demonstrate a capacity to look through the objectivizing, few-for-many logics that Žižek claims are the Real of modern warfare.

The PlayStation Mentality

I will be the first to acknowledge that this is probably not how most will play the *Modern Warfare* series. Many skip the story mode altogether in favor of the multiplayer offerings. Those who do play the story are unlikely to think twice about dispensing the monitor-watching guard even after the face-to-face knifing of his colleague in the previous scene. Those who feel uncomfortable participating in "No Russian" are still unlikely to draw connections between the fate of some NPCs and visual feedback from cameras mounted on Predator drones.

Even so, the ability to make those connections is what is at stake in recognizing the place of the videogamer within today's military-entertainment complex. While it may be easy to shrug off the *Modern Warfare* series as "just games," thereby justifying whatever on-screen atrocities are visited on inconsequential, infinitely respawing NPCs, the ability to do so relies on the informatic, objectivized logic that is also at play in contemporary digitally mediated warfare, "the very pillars that prop those systems up."[39] Playing a *Modern Warfare* game thus bears more than a metaphorical relationship to the actual modern warfare technologies and practices it represents on-screen.

FIGURE 7.12. Silhouettes of non-playable characters as viewed through the AC-130 targeting interface during the "Death from Above" level in Infinity Ward's *Call of Duty 4: Modern Warfare*.

This is not to say that the enemy silhouettes scurrying across our (simu-lated) AC-130 targeting display correspond to real human lives. In remedi-ated YouTube videos or newsreel footage of actual AC-130 attacks, however, they do. As we increasingly live our lives in online environments and interact with one another through screens of various sizes, it is of utmost importance that we are able to recognize in the digital display the weight and value of human life, even if all we ever know is the outline of a pixelated silhouette.

CODA

The Rock of the Virtual

Violence in *Blood Meridian* and *Red Dead Redemption*

Violence became central to this book in ways I did not anticipate. When I first met with my eventual editor to discuss the working manuscript, he pointed out to me that each chapter revolves around scenes of graphic violence: the school shooting at Columbine, the random murder of a family in Kansas, the execution animations in a military first-person shooter. Though this had not been my initial aim, my investigation into the exchanges between the virtual and the actual kept returning to moments of traumatic violence.

To conclude this study of fiction in wired culture, I attempt to reflect on what violence has meant to this project. Through a brief juxtaposition of two more fictions—Rockstar San Diego's *Red Dead Redemption* (Rockstar Games, 2010) and one of its clear source texts, Cormac McCarthy's 1985 novel *Blood Meridian*—I will articulate a number of questions this study has raised about virtuality, interactivity, complicity, and agency. Though I do not expect to come away with clear answers, these lingering issues have broad implications not only for the study of videogames and literature but for wired culture at large.

First, a scene from *Red Dead Redemption,* a game about a reformed outlaw, John Marston, whose wife and child are held by the government until Marston apprehends or kills the leaders of his former gang. In an early-game mission titled "Spare the Rod, Spoil the Bandit," Marston posses with a small-town marshal to track a group of bandits, who have been "getting drunk and murdering settlers." The deputies elaborate with a gruesome report of the previous night's attack on Ridgewood Farm: "They burnt the place down, killed the men, burning most of them alive, and raped the women. The women folk then got their throats slit. One of them survived and walked in here this morning." Riding out, the posse finds a trail of dead bodies and a series of decimated campsites, leading all the way to Ridgewood.

Arriving at the farm, the posse finds it empty, absent signs of life. The player guides Marston to search the site, soon finding a trail of blood leading to a boarded-up barn. Inside the player finds a horrific scene—another, larger pile of bodies, a man strung up, hanging naked from the rafters. From an over-the-shoulder shot to a reverse-angle reaction shot, the party confirms for the viewer the horror of the scene. A lone survivor impossibly emerges and informs us that the bandits are in the farmhouse with more survivors. The cutscene closes by panning up in to a close-up of the hanging, naked corpse.

How are we to make sense of this virtual slaughter? The game is quite clear: this is supposed to be egregious, gratuitous violence. But is that how the player experiences it?

The player discovers not merely one decimated campsite, but many. The massacre is repeated, creating a protracted slaughter leading from one crime scene to the next. Is this repetition emblematic of the player's desensitization

FIGURE C.1. Marston and crew find a pile of dead bodies in Rockstar San Diego's *Red Dead Redemption*.

FIGURE C.2. The crew opens the barn to find more bodies and a naked corpse hanged from the rafters in Rockstar San Diego's *Red Dead Redemption*. The horror of the scene is confirmed by the reverse-angle reaction shot of Marston and crew. The angle is reversed again to a perspectival shot from Marston's position, giving players a close-up view of the carnage.

toward violence, or does it reproduce it? Or might the compiling of gore resensitize these virtualities? At no point were these NPCs ever alive and meandering through even the procedurally generated AI everyday. They exist only ever here, corpses piled among the rocks, anchoring a violent landscape of play. Does the player mourn the death of these unmet NPCs, these bloody props? Do our encounters with scattered, mangled bodies, this naked hanging corpse, ever give over to the traumatic? Can we encounter in virtual violence the rock of the real?

Regarding the repeated images of car crash victims in Andy Warhol's *Ambulance Disaster* (1963) and *White Burning Car III* (1963), Hal Foster remarks that repetition *"screens"* or mediates the viewer's access to the real event.[1] Foregrounding the artifice of the image distances the viewer. At the same time, however, the repetition *"points* to the real." The artificial image itself can produce its own "second order of trauma" whereby the real ruptures the initial screen and the viewer is *"touched* by an image."[2] Foster attributes this to Warhol's artistic technique. Mark Hansen, however, suggests it may be the inevitable effect of living in wired culture. Mediation has become so ubiquitous and inexorable that it constitutes the "bedrock on which a belief in reality can be founded."[3] Does this sequence from *Red Dead Redemption* offer us such a rock? Does this stylized violence touch us, bring us in contact with the trauma of the real? Or merely screen violence?

To gain some perspective on these questions, let us compare the virtual violence of *Red Dead Redemption* to that of *Blood Meridian*. Here is one extended sentence from the kid's first encounter with the Comanches:

> Now driving in a wild frieze of headlong horses with eyes walled and teeth cropped and naked riders with clusters of arrows clenched in their jaws and their shields winking in the dust and up the far side of the ruined ranks in a piping of boneflutes and dropping down off the sides of their mounts with one heel hung in the withers strap and their short bows flexing beneath the outstretched necks of the ponies until they had circled the company and cut their ranks in two and then rising up again like funhouse figures, some with nightmare faces painted on their breasts, riding down the unhorsed Saxons and spearing and clubbing them and leaping from their mounts with knives and running about on the ground with a peculiar bandylegged trot like creatures

driven to alien forms of locomotion and stripping the clothes from the dead
and seizing them up by the hair and passing their blades about the skulls of the
living and the dead alike and snatching aloft the bloody wigs and hacking and
chopping at the naked bodies, ripping off limbs, heads, gutting the strange
white torsos and holding up great handfuls of viscera, genitals, some of the
savages so slathered up with gore they might have rolled in it like dogs and
some who fell upon the dying and sodomized them with loud cries to their
fellows.[4]

How are we to engage with such passages?

Harold Bloom admits that he found the violence in *Blood Meridian* so
repulsive he failed to finish reading the book on two separate occasions. Even
so, he implores readers to persist as the novel's "magnificence—its language,
landscape, persons, and conceptions—at last transcends the violence."[5] It is
hard to imagine a videogame receiving such a generous reading of its blood
and gore.

Timothy Parrish as well writes that the characters of *Blood Meridian* "commit acts which one might call unspeakable in their atrocity if McCarthy did
not render these acts with a poetic force unsurpassed in all of American fiction."[6] He observes that McCarthy's Western novels "accept violence as a
condition of being alive and they are not simply (and easily) critiquing a
cartoonish version of an exceptionalist American history."[7]

Blood Meridian neither romanticizes nor moralizes the violence that
shaped the American West and its mythology. Instead, drawing on the
nineteenth-century memoirs of Samuel Chamberlain, the novel describes
actual historical events accurately in order to, as Parrish puts it, "see if they
mean anything other than the primal surge of power experienced during their
expression."

But as a result, Steven Shaviro argues, it offers readers no self-conscious
position and no "curative discharge of fear and pity."[8] The book places us
in the position of Glanton's murderous gang—as McCarthy puts it, given
over "entire to the blood of war" (331)—as "we too are implicated in the
savage spectacle."[9] "Our pulses quicken," Shaviro writes, as "'considerations
of equity and rectitude and moral right [are] rendered void and without
warrant,' subsumed in the trials of war."[10] Shaviro describes our reading as a

"euphoric and exhilarating" reiteration of "violent, sacrificial, self-consuming ritual upon which our civilization is founded."

Through the beauty and artistry of language, readers become complicit with the cycles of violence on which the American West and its mythos were founded. McCarthy's novel simultaneously undoes the romantic Western imaginary and affirms it, returning that kernel of the real—the brutal settling of the Western frontier—mediated by McCarthy's seductive language, which warrants acceptance and enjoyment.

But is this the same complicity with violence as when we play violent games, in which, to quote Chief Justice John Roberts in *Brown v. Electronic Merchants Association*, the player is "doing the killing, doing the maiming"?[11] Are we implicated in the unspeakable horrors of manifest destiny when playing *Red Dead Redemption*? How does reading a fictionalized narrative of historical violence compare to playing a videogame it inspired? Shaviro states, "The writing of *Blood Meridian* is a catastrophic act of witness, embracing the real by tracing it in gore."[12] If that is what a book can do, what would it mean to think of or play videogames—a medium defined as action—in the same way?

These questions take on urgency beyond just videogaming, though. Our digital devices and the virtual environments they generate put us in touch with real violences, both local and global: Coltan farming, gold farming, the digital divide, the military-entertainment complex, cyberbullying, the Arab Spring, ISIS, NSA surveillance, GamerGate, and so on. These violences circulate through the virtual environments in which we conduct our wired lives. Quite beyond anything like gory content, the simple, real-world act of using digital media occurs in relation to these contexts. But how do we understand this participation? How do these virtual worlds join our banal digital media use to real violences?

This book has focused on mixed realism, or the synchronicity of virtual and material realms. Videogames have been particularly illustrative of this concept because of the way they use narratives to reframe the act of playing them. In doing so, videogames fold our actions in fictional worlds into all sorts of real social, political, and ethical circumstances.

Red Dead Redemption, for instance, takes place a few years after *Blood Meridian* but also concerns the transition to a settled, civilized West. Where it differs markedly in emphasis is in its fixation on new technologies. Throughout the game characters remark on how the train has changed the landscape, on the new-fangled horseless carriages, on telephones.

In this way, the game signals that it is not merely historical but reflects on the contemporary moment in which it is played as well, a moment of significant cultural transition ushered forward by technological developments, like videogames. Thus the questions the game asks of Marston about the meaning and morality of his actions apply in some degree to the player as well: a mixed reality. Given our situatedness in this media ecology, what does it mean to kill so many (virtual) outlaws?

Red Dead Redemption fails to offer a clear moral compass, the kind of action-consequence structures that gaming's critics always wish will follow in-game violence. Scenes like the one above set Marston up as transitioning from outlaw to homesteader, clearing the West of wanton violence, making it safe for home and family, both his own and the coming civilized populations. Yet Marston's supposedly justified violence is constantly called into question. After discovering another site of random slaughter, Bonnie McFarlane expresses her disgust at Marston's murderous past and chides him for trying to justify it with "twisted morality": "The outlaw with a code? How

FIGURE C.3. This shot from the opening cutscene of Rockstar San Diego's *Red Dead Redemption* lingers on an automobile, setting up the theme of new technologies.

wonderfully romantic! The reluctant murderer, the noble criminal. There's nothing more depressing than a man who's found a way to think the bad into good." In moments like these the game refuses to let us see Marston as acting through moral rectitude, suggesting that Marston is not so different from the outlaws he hunts.

Later on in the mission "Demon Drink," for instance, Marston must set fire to Tesoro Azul, enabling Allende's men to deliver the town's women to Colonel Allende, all in hopes that he might learn the location of the outlaws he seeks and be able to return to his family. The player as Marston might recognize that his quest has brought him to the same state as the roving gangs that attacked Ridgewood. This is to be a moment of egregious violence, where the player is supposed to feel uncomfortable about participating in the virtual slaughter. Confronted by the old gunslinger Landon Ricketts for his inconsistency, Marston espouses the objectivized logic of a videogame: "I must find the two men, how I do it is no concern of yours."

In the end, though, this is an open-world sandbox by Rockstar, the makers of the *Grand Theft Auto* series, and so it affords all manner of gratuitous, verging on silly, interactive violence. The game's efforts to figure the character of Marston as opposed to the chaotic, destructive impulses indulged

FIGURE C.4. In "The Demon Drink" level of Rockstar San Diego's *Red Dead Redemption* Marston must set fire to a number of houses in the village of Tesoro Azul.

by Rockstar's other games, stretch the bounds of ludo-narrative plausibility. This is, after all, just a game, as my students often say, and these are only arrangements of pixels. The violences perpetrated on-screen for the player's amusement are not real, nor do they carry the weight of what they represent. In fact, that is part of their appeal: they are meaningless, insignificant, infinitely respawnable. The horrific acts in which we as players participate are only skins for rule sets, trading on the stakes of actual violence in order to give significance to ephemeral digital objects and the repetition of button presses. In this way, as McCarthy's Judge Holden would say, the game "aspires to the condition of war" (261). For the judge, though games do not carry the stakes of violence, they do exhibit the same decisiveness.

"War," Judge Holden concludes, "is the ultimate game because war is at last a forcing of the unity of existence." Amid the wanton brutality of the West, the decisiveness of violence offers the only stable truth, the only bedrock on which can be built a belief in reality: "Decisions of life and death, of what shall be and what shall not, beggar all question of right. In elections of these magnitudes are all lesser ones subsumed, moral, spiritual, natural." For this reason, "it makes no difference what men think of war, said the judge. War endures. As well ask men what they think of stone" (259).

For Judge Holden "the universe is no narrow thing," vast beyond all comprehension and therefore dangerous: "These anonymous creatures, he said, may seem little or nothing in the world. Yet the smallest crumb can devour us. Any smallest thing beneath yon rock out of men's knowing" (256, 207). The only knowledge that matters here, Parrish writes, "is the difference that separates the living and the dead and the only way to truly experience the power of this knowledge is through killing someone else."[13] Partaking in violence, enacting the decisiveness of war, is for the judge a way to impose one's will, to be the determiner of one's own fate: "But the man who sets himself the task of singling out the thread of order from the tapestry will by that decision alone have taken charge of the world and it is only by such taking charge that he will effect a way to dictate the terms of his own fate" (208).

We can read the judge's perspective on war and existence into the playing of *Red Dead Redemption*. Marston, too, finds himself in a savage frontier, where Bonnie's moralizing is cut short by the discovery that Williamson's gang has set her barn on fire. The binary expression of alive or dead overrides questions of moral treatment of the NPCs we encounter. Indeed, procedurally generated encounters introduce the player's Marston to NPCs who will attempt to rob him, steal his horse, or kill him.

Beyond the objectivized survivalism of gameplay, the whole landscape and all within it is there for the player to deal with as she desires. This is, in fact, what has long been celebrated about Rockstar's games—their capacity to grant players the freedom to play by their own designs, to express their own will within a broad and varied interactive environment. Yet this freedom depends on a judge-like attitude toward the virtual world. The ability to impose one's will on the non-playable inhabitants of *Red Dead Redemption* always reminds me of a sequence from *Blood Meridian* in which the judge purchases from a small boy two puppies, which he then tosses into the river where his urinating comrade shoots them. McCarthy, of course, describes the rivulets of there blood mixing with the rolling river beautifully.

Red Dead Redemption, again, is just a game. Even so, it embodies or solicits a kind of nihilism that is worrisome if generalized. Even if restricted to games and the virtual realm, as I discussed earlier, ever more of contemporary social life is conducted in digital environments. It is increasingly important to be

FIGURE C.5. More dead bodies in Rockstar San Diego's *Red Dead Redemption*, this time just outside Bonnie MacFarlane's ranch. When the player, as Marston, and Bonnie return to the ranch, they find the barn has been set on fire.

able to recognize humanity in the on-screen display, and in this way join online and offline contexts in a "unity of existence."

The McCarthy of *Blood Meridian* does not always align with Judge Holden's philosophies. McCarthy seems to affirm the judge's assessment of reality: "This desert upon which so many have been broken is vast and calls for largeness of heart but it is also ultimately empty. It is hard, it is barren. Its very nature is stone" (344). At points, though, McCarthy grows weary of the violence. In a rare instance of second-person address, the narrator remarks, "How else could it be? How these things end," before describing with a generic distance yet another deadly bar fight (43). Moments like these suggest the judge's is merely one interpretation of this empty desert. In fact, just prior to the judge's speech on war and games, McCarthy offers us an alternative.

A few days out from Tucson, Glanton's crew discovers a crucified Apache, the "mummied corpse hung from the cross tree with its mouth gaped in a raw hole," and "they rode on" (258). As the passage continues, it implies that this remainder of violence put the landscape in perspective:

> The horses trudged sullenly the alien ground and the round earth rolled beneath them silently milling the greater void wherein they were contained. In the neuter austerity of that terrain all phenomena were bequeathed a strange

FIGURE C.6. Marston compliments his son, Jack, in Rockstar San Diego's *Red Dead Redemption*.

equality and no one thing nor spider nor stone nor blade of grass could put
forth claim to precedence. The very clarity of those articles belied their familiarity, for the eye predicates the whole on some feature or part and here was
nothing more luminous than another and nothing more enshadowed and in
the optical democracy of such landscapes all preference is made whimsical
and a man and a rock become endowed with unguessed kinships. (258–59)

Rather than the imposition of one's will on the void, we might instead see
in *Red Dead Redemption* an opportunity, even within the violence, to seek
these "unguessed kinships."

We might, for example, come to care for a particular horse, despite the
fact that it is easily replaced with an identical copy. That brief feeling of loss
at the elimination of a digital object speaks to a capacity to see past objectivized logics of the game. Though somewhat saccharine, the last few missions
in which the player teaches Marston's son to hunt manage to hang emotions
on an NPC we meet for less than an hour of gameplay. It provides a meaningful context for the game's open-world postscript in which we take control
of a matured Jack and might seek revenge for John's death.

Though certainly not a matter of true life and death, there are stakes in
finding significance and connection with an arrangement of pixels. As digital

FIGURE C.7. Rockstar San Diego's *Red Dead Redemption*.

media technologies infiltrate all aspects of daily life it is increasingly important for us to be able to articulate what is at hazard.

We, too, find ourselves in a new landscape, a digital media ecology familiar yet strange. Like the riders, our medial terrain confronts us with a crisis
of interpretive uncertainty. Automated news aggregators inform us about
social revolutions playing out on social media sites where friends demand
"pics or shut the fuck up."[14] The catfishing of a college football star is a
national scandal, while college students around the country rally against the
use of African children as soldiers they saw in a documentary posted to You-
Tube.[15] The virtualities of media are increasingly the way in which we come
to know about and interact with the world, and our reliance on this mediated world has both large- and small-scale consequences. After witnessing
planes fly into the World Trade Center towers live on morning talk shows,
a nation watches Colin Powell hold up grainy satellite images as he argues
for expanding military operations in the Middle East.[16] Over ten years later,
the NSA looks for indicators of terrorist activities by combing through data
from online search providers, data used and sold by those companies to build
profiles that customize results and target products to the user who goes online
looking for recommendations.[17]

Ours is a mixed reality, in which big and small screens blend virtual environments into everyday life, and old binaries dissolve as the virtual and the
actual take on a "strange equality." In the great void, "unguessed kinships" are
emerging between man and rock, user and avatar. Even if we are still learning
to read them.

ACKNOWLEDGMENTS

As with all books, this one couldn't have happened without the work, support, and inspiration of numerous people.

I would like to thank the University of Minnesota Press and the Electronic Mediations series editors for accepting this work into their prestigious collection. Thank you to my anonymous peer-review readers; their incisive comments made this a better book. Thanks go to Susan Clements for her work on the index. To my editor, Doug Armato, thank you for believing in this project from our first meeting in Seattle through the long revision process.

Thank you to my professors, classmates, students, and friends at the University of Washington where this project first took root. I am most grateful for the early feedback I received on these ideas from Leroy Searle, Phillip Thurtle, and especially Brian Reed, who often understood how this project was coming together before I did. The Critical Gaming Project and its initiator, Terry Schenold, the Comparative History of Ideas Program, and the Simpson Center for the Humanities provided invaluable forums and opportunities for the humanistic study of digital games. To my friend and collaborator Ed Chang, thank you for sharing your work and friendship with me.

I am grateful to Loyola University New Orleans for its continued and generous support of my research. Thank you to my marvelous colleagues and students in the English department for welcoming me and my digital scholarship into their community. In particular, thank you to my faculty mentor

John Sebastian for helping me navigate the profession, and to my student research assistant Richard O'Brien for handling so much detail work while I was face-deep in revisions. Special thanks go to Chris Schaberg, who helped me work over nearly this entire book: you give me the confidence to be a better writer. To Brian Sullivan, thank you for your tireless advocacy for digital humanities, for your input on this project, and for your friendship.

Finally, thank you to my family for their continued love and support. To my partner, Lindsay, thank you for letting me borrow your GameCube and for so much more.

NOTES

Introduction

1. William Gibson, *Spook Country* (New York: Penguin, 2008), 64.

2. Pierre Lévy, *Becoming Virtual: Reality in the Digital Age*, trans. Robert Bononno (New York: Plenum Trade, 1998), 16. Lévy presents an excellent examination of how "the virtual" as a form of being relates to digital technologies. For the purposes of this book, I will be bracketing his "strict," philosophical definition as I discuss something closer to what Theodor Nelson referred to as "virtuality." In "Interactive Systems and the Design of Virtuality," *Creative Computing* 6, no. 11 (1980), Nelson calls the virtual a "structure of seeming," by which he means the way an application of paint to canvas invokes what he would call the "conceptual feel" of a landscape (57). As will become swiftly apparent, however, I reject Nelson's understanding of the "virtual" as the "opposite of 'real'" and the implication that "implementation details" are "irrelevant." I discuss the significance of Nelson's conceptualization of virtuality for the legacy of first-generation virtuality research in the next chapter. For now, let "the virtual" simply indicate media-generated and media-dependent, nonphysical objects and environments.

3. Wendy Hui Kyong Chun, *Control and Freedom: Power and Paranoia in the Age of Fiber Optics* (Cambridge, Mass.: MIT Press, 2006), 42–43. Chun explains that Gibson's cyberspace was central to the marketing of the Internet, and digital technologies more generally, as "an endless space for individualism and/or capitalism, as an endless freedom frontier." Cyberspace is, thus, "science fiction" not merely because of its literary origins, but because it mapped on to real technologies, blending fiction with science.

4. Edward Castronova, *Synthetic Worlds: The Business and Culture of Online Games* (Chicago: University of Chicago Press, 2005), 286.

5. Louis Budd, "The American Background," in *The Cambridge Companion to American Realism and Naturalism: From Howells to London*, ed. Donald Pizer (Cambridge, U.K.: Cambridge University Press, 1995), 37.

6. Marie-Laure Ryan, *Narrative as Virtual Reality: Immersion and Interactivity in Literature and Electronic Media* (Baltimore: Johns Hopkins University Press, 2003).

7. Brian McHale, *Postmodernist Fiction* (New York: Methuen, 1987).

8. Marie-Laure Ryan, "Immersion vs. Interactivity: Virtual Reality and Literary Theory," *Postmodern Culture* 5, no. 1 (1994): http://muse.jhu.edu/article/27495.

9. Qtd. in Mike Musgrove, "How Real Is Too Real?" *Washington Post*, January 18, 2007, http://www.washingtonpost.com/wp-dyn/content/article/2007/01/17/AR2007011702051.html.

10. Danny Ledonne, "Artist's Statement: A Meditation on *Super Columbine Massacre RPG!*" April 9, 2011, http://www.columbinegame.com/statement.htm.

11. For an example of scholarship connecting the events at Columbine to overexposure to videogames, see J. J. Block, "Lessons from Columbine: Virtual and Real Rage," *American Journal of Forensic Psychiatry* 28, no. 2 (2007): 5–34.

12. Ian Bogost, "Columbine RPG," *Water Cooler Games*, May 3, 2006, http://www.bogost.com/watercoolergames/archives/columbine_rpg.shtml.

13. For more on how the AP picked up *Super Columbine Massacre RPG!* see Ian Bogost, "Columbine, Videogames as Expression, and Ineffability." *Water Cooler Games*, May 21, 2006, http://www.bogost.com/watercoolergames/archives/columbine_video.shtml.

14. See Patrick Dugan, "Soapbox: Why You Owe the Columbine RPG," *Gamasutra*, March 13, 2007, http://www.gamasutra.com/view/feature/1699/soapbox_why_you_owe_the_columbine_.php.

15. Emru Townsend, "The 10 Worst Games of All Time," *PC World*, October 23, 2006, http://www.pcworld.com/article/127579/article.html. The title ranked third on the list was *Custer's Revenge* (Mystique, 1982).

16. Peter Baxter, the Slamdance festival founder, was originally quoted in Brian Crecente, "Slamdance Unplugs Columbine Video Game," *Rocky Mountain News*, January 6, 2007. For more on the removal of *Super Columbine Massacre RPG!* from the competition see Brian Crecente, "Exclusive: Columbine Game Kicked from Competition," *Kotaku*, January 5, 2007, http://kotaku.com/226272/exclusive-columbine-game-kicked-from-competition.

17. Qtd. in Associated Press, "Columbine Video Game Draws Relatives' Ire," *USA Today*, May 17, 2006, http://usatoday30.usatoday.com/tech/gaming/2006-05-17-columbine-game_x.htm.

18. For example, see Christine Laue, "Violent Video Games Again in Cross Hairs," *Omaha World-Herald*, September 19, 2006.

19. Qtd. in Brodie Fenlon, "Game Creator Says He's Sorry, but Doesn't Believe Columbine Simulation behind Montreal Murder," *Toronto Sun*, September 15, 2006, from Smith's website, http://www.thefreeradical.ca/videoGames/articlesOnDawson CollegeShootings.html.

20. Jesper Juul, *Half-Real: Video Games between Real Rules and Fictional Worlds* (Cambridge, Mass.: MIT Press, 2005), 1.

21. The full speech appears on YouTube, posted by "The White House," as "President Obama Makes a Statement on the Shooting in Newtown, Connecticut," December 14, 2012, http://youtu.be/mIAoW69U2_Y.

22. See Lawrence Kutner and Cheryl Olson, *Grand Theft Childhood: The Surprising Truth about Violent Video Games and What Parents Can Do* (New York: Simon & Schuster, 2008).

23. TheHalfrican, "Violent Video Games? Lanza Played *Dynasty Warriors*," *Daily Kos*, December 17, 2012, http://www.dailykos.com/story/2012/12/17/1171298/-Violent-Video-Games-Lanza-played-Dynasty-Warriors.

24. Leigh Ann Caldwell, "Obama Sets Up Gun Violence Task Force," *CBS News*, December 19, 2012, http://www.cbsnews.com/8301-250_162-57560044/obama-sets-up-gun-violence-task-force/.

25. Steve Holland and Roberta Rampton, "NRA, Video Game Makers to Meet with Biden Gun Task Force This Week," *Reuters*, January 8, 2013, http://www.reuters.com/article/2013/01/08/us-usa-guns-nra-idUSBRE9070TT20130108.

26. *Brown v. Entertainment Merchants Association*, 564 U.S. 08-1448 (2010), http://www.supremecourt.gov/oral_arguments/argument_transcripts/08-1448.pdf.

27. Ibid.

28. See Ian Bogost, "Why Debates about Video Games Aren't Really about Video Games," *Kotaku*, August 1, 2011, http://kotaku.com/5826559/why-debates-about-video-games-arent-about-video-games.

29. The full E3 demonstration introduction of the *Milo* game and Project Natal can be viewed on YouTube, uploaded by "24/7 GAMES," as "E3 2009—Project Natal—Milo Demo with Peter Molyneux 720p HD," June 2, 2009, http://youtu.be/yDvHlwN vXaM.

30. Ryan, *Narrative as Virtual Reality*, 57.

31. One might also point here to recent interest in the Oculus Rift, as the media hype surrounding this head-mounted VR display now recalls, in nearly identical language, the hype surrounding virtual reality technologies in the 1990s. See, the suite of articles titled "The Rise and Fall and Rise of Virtual Reality" on *The Verge* website, http://www.theverge.com/a/virtual-reality.

178 NOTES TO INTRODUCTION

32. See N. Katherine Hayles, "Condition of Virtuality," in *The Digital Dialectic: New Essays on New Media*, ed. Peter Lunenfeld (Cambridge, Mass.: MIT Press, 2000), 69–95.

33. Matthew Kirschenbaum, *Mechanisms: New Media and the Forensic Imagination* (Cambridge, Mass.: MIT Press, 2008), 42. Kirschenbaum discusses Hayles as one of numerous examples, "year to year," of medial ideology.

34. Ian Bogost, "Videogames Are a Mess," address delivered at the annual conference of the Digital Games Research Association, Uxbridge, U.K., September 1–4, 2009, http://www.bogost.com/writing/videogames_are_a_mess.shtml.

35. See Wendy Hui Kyong Chun, *Programmed Visions: Software and Memory* (Cambridge, Mass.: MIT Press, 2011).

36. Dugan, "Soapbox."

37. Musgrove, "How Real Is Too Real?"

38. Some of the figures appearing in the "Island of Lost Souls" room include Socrates, Ronald Reagan, Malcolm X, a Manhattan Project scientist, JonBenét Ramsey, John Lennon, Santa Claus, Darth Vader, Bart Simpson, Super Mario, Pokémon, a ninja, a *Challenger* astronaut, and Mega Man. Other notable appearances in hell include Nietzsche, who has his own room, and Satan from the television series *South Park*, who serves as the game's final boss, or last and most challenging enemy.

39. Dugan, "Soapbox."

40. Robert Mitchell, *Bioart and the Vitality of Media* (Seattle: University of Washington Press, 2010), 124. Mitchell, in fact, mentions "the digitization that computing technologies make possible" as another potential form of "vital media."

41. Beatriz da Costa, *Transgenic Bacteria Release Machine*, 2001–3.

42. David Foster Wallace, *Infinite Jest* (New York: Little, Brown, 1996).

43. For more in-depth discussion of social media's role in the Arab Spring, see Gadi Wolfsfeld, Elad Segev, and Tamir Sheafer, "Social Media and the Arab Spring: Politics Comes First," *International Journal of Press/Politics* 18, no. 2 (2013): 115–37.

44. "Metro (Design Language)," *Wikipedia*, May 21, 2013, http://en.wikipedia.org/w/index.php?title=Metro_(design_language)&oldid=554701155.

45. Alain Badiou, *The Century*, trans. Alberto Toscano (Malden, Mass.: Polity, 2007).

46. Constance Steinkuehler, "The Mangle of Play," *Games and Culture* 1, no. 3 (2006): 199–213; Alexander Galloway, *Gaming: Essays on Algorithmic Culture* (Minneapolis: University of Minnesota Press, 2006), 105; Bogost, "Videogames Are a Mess."

47. Linda Hutcheon, *Narcissistic Narrative: The Metafictional Paradox* (Waterloo, Ont.: Wilfrid Laurier University Press, 1980), 5.

48. Janet H. Murray, *Hamlet on the Holodeck: The Future of Narrative in Cyberspace* (Cambridge, Mass.: MIT Press, 1998), 98.

1. Immersive Fictions in the Dot-com Era

1. Pierre Lévy, *Becoming Virtual: Reality in the Digital Age*, trans. Robert Bononno (New York: Plenum Trade, 1998), 16.

2. The virtual for Lévy is defined as tending toward the actual. His simple example is the seed (24). Any particular seed, as a real phenomenon, is a small kernel, a singular instantiation of one of the multitude of possible seed-beings. In its capacity to take root and grow, this singular kernel is a virtual tree. The tree-tending quality of a seed is not "false, illusory, or imaginary"; rather, its capacity for becoming a tree is made up of cotemporaneous aspects of a polyvalent profile of being-seed, becoming-tree.

3. Lilly Wachowski and Lana Wachowski, *The Matrix* (Warner Bros., 1999).

4. Theodor Nelson, "Interactive Systems and the Design of Virtuality," *Creative Computing* 6, no. 11 (1980): 57. The issue can be retrieved from https://archive.org/details/creativecomputing-1980-11.

5. The dot-com bubble is often cited as beginning in 1993 when the Mosaic browser made the World Wide Web accessible and popular with the general public. See Robert Reid, *The Architects of the Web: 1,000 Days That Built the Future of Business* (New York: Wiley, 1997). Following low interest rates in 1998–99, a proliferation of Internet-based start-up companies opened to public trading. Such trading peaked in the first quarter of 2000 and sharply declined through the rest of that year, indicating that the bubble had burst. The following year saw continued decline as companies burned through what remained of their venture capital. The events of September 11, 2001, brought a general economic slowdown that marked the close of the dot-com era.

6. For a discussion of Plato, virtuality, and videogames, see Alexander Galloway, "Philosophy and Games," audio recording, NYU Game Center Lecture Series, 2009–10, http://gamecenter.nyu.edu/nyu-game-center-lecture-series-philosophy-and-games/.

7. Lévy, *Becoming Virtual*, 16.

8. Edward Castronova, *Synthetic Worlds: The Business and Culture of Online Games* (Chicago: University of Chicago Press, 2005), 286.

9. Frank Biocca, Taeyong Kim, and Mark Levy, "The Vision of Virtual Reality," in *Communication in the Age of Virtual Reality*, ed. Frank Biocca and Mark Levy (Hillsdale, N.J.: Lawrence Erlbaum Associates), 4.

10. Howard Rheingold, *Virtual Reality: The Revolutionary Technology of Computer-Generated Artificial Worlds—and How It Promises to Transform Society* (New York: Summit Books, 1991), 17.

11. Ron Wodaski, *Virtual Reality Madness!* (Carmel, Ind.: Sams Publishing, 1993), 79.

12. Ken Pimentel and Kevin Teixeira, *Virtual Reality: Through the New Looking Glass* (New York: Intel/Windcrest, 1993), 15.

13. Janet Murray, *Hamlet on the Holodeck: The Future of Narrative in Cyberspace* (Cambridge, Mass.: MIT Press, 1998). The holodeck appears in numerous episodes of *Star Trek: The Next Generation*, including the series pilot. See "Encounter at Farpoint," *Star Trek: The Next Generation*, September 28, 1987.

14. Murray, *Hamlet on the Holodeck*, 98.

15. The model of immersion that formed the basis for comparison here is what Gordon Calleja identifies as "immersion as transportation," significantly distinguished from "immersion as absorption." See *In-Game: From Immersion to Incorporation* (Cambridge, Mass.: MIT Press, 2011), 28. I wholeheartedly agree that continued generic use of the term "immersion" has produced confusion in the literature. My concern here is less with immersion per se than with the way assumptions about how immersion perpetuates an ontological opposition between the virtual and the real, which, for simplicity, I will refer to as the *immersive binary*.

16. Murray, *Hamlet on the Holodeck*, 98.

17. Pimentel and Teixeira, *Virtual Reality*, 15.

18. Nelson, "Interactive Systems and the Design of Virtuality," 57.

19. Castronova, *Synthetic Worlds*, 285.

20. Frank Biocca and Ben Delaney, "Immersive Virtual Reality Technology," in *Communication in the Age of Virtual Reality*, ed. Frank Biocca and Mark Levy (Hillsdale, N.J.: Lawrence Erlbaum Associates, 1995), 57n1.

21. Not only does the technology in *The Matrix* resemble 1990s VR, the film is explicit about the real/virtual binary informing its concept of immersion. For example, when Cypher agrees to betray Morpheus over dinner with Agent Smith, he remarks, "I know that this steak doesn't exist. I know when I put it in my mouth, the Matrix is telling my brain that it is juicy and delicious." His physically plugged-in body is reclining in a chair with a cord running from the neck, not eating anything at all, as the simulation technology has replaced those senses with computer-generated ones. The terms of his betrayal, then, to be reinserted into the Matrix, is a request not merely to be hooked up to the machine but to also give up awareness of his embodiment—or, as he puts it succinctly, "Ignorance is bliss."

22. Marie-Laure Ryan, *Narrative as Virtual Reality: Immersion and Interactivity in Literature and Electronic Media* (Baltimore: Johns Hopkins University Press, 2003), 58.

23. Murray, *Hamlet on the Holodeck*, 99–100. Citing the work of the child psychologist D. W. Winnicott on "transitional objects" and their role in make-believe, Murray explains that the "threshold experiences" offered by computer environments and narratives depend on the fact that the virtual is not real. For immersion to work, "we have to keep the virtual world 'real' by keeping it 'not there.'" In other words, we can have these threshold experiences as long as the threshold remains intact, with the really real on one side and the virtually real on the other.

24. Castronova, *Synthetic Worlds*, 286.

25. According to Castronova, this "standardized vision of VR" involves "a single person in a special room, wearing a big helmet, her arms and legs wired up to something mobile."

26. Ryan, *Narrative as Virtual Reality*, 57.

27. Ryan, "Immersion vs. Interactivity: Virtual Reality and Literary Theory," *Postmodern Culture* 5, no. 1 (1994): http://muse.jhu.edu/journals/postmodern_culture/v 005/5.1ryan.html.

28. Pimentel and Teixeira, *Virtual Reality*, 11.

29. Ryan, "Immersion vs. Interactivity."

30. Frank Biocca, "Virtual Reality Technology: A Tutorial," *Journal of Communication* 42, no. 4 (1992): 25.

31. Ryan, "Immersion vs. Interactivity."

32. Ryan argues that, unlike VR, which unites immersion and interactivity by allowing subjects to engage the virtual world physically, literature "offers a choice between the cerebral [mental interaction with language] and the corporeal [the sense of immersed presence]" (*Narrative as Virtual Reality*, 355). A similar immersive ultimatum appears in videogame scholarship; this will be discussed in chapter 3.

33. Ryan, "Immersion vs. Interactivity."

34. Ryan, *Narrative as Virtual Reality*, 159.

35. Ryan treats this concept at length in "Fictional Recentering," in *Possible Worlds, Artificial Intelligence, and Narrative Theory* (Bloomington: Indiana University Press, 1992), 21–30.

36. For this reason, the metafictional techniques prominent in the twentieth century fail to support immersive reading in Ryan's system, as self-reference is a form of "demystification" ("Immersion vs. Interactivity"): "By overtly recognizing the constructed, imaginary nature of the textual world, metafiction reclaims our 'native reality' as ontological center and reverts to the status of nonfictional discourse about nonactual possible worlds."

37. Ryan, *Narrative as Virtual Reality*, 158.

38. Ibid., 157.

39. The supposed "transparency" of the realist style has long been contested. See, for example, Amy Kaplan, *The Social Construction of American Realism* (Chicago: University of Chicago Press, 1992); and Alan Trachtenberg, "Fictions of the Real," in *The Incorporation of America: Culture and Society in the Gilded Age* (New York: Hill and Wang, 2007), 182–207. Though Ryan recognizes these objections, she argues that they are symptomatic of modern modes of criticism rather than reflective of reading practices. She writes, "The discrepancy between mode of narration and mimetic claim wasn't noticed until the development of narratology and linguistic pragmatics" (*Narrative as Virtual Reality*, 159).

40. Ibid., 58–59.

41. Ryan, *Possible Worlds*, 34.

42. In Ryan's system of accessibility relations, "true fiction" ranks just below accurate nonfiction, which are "works of history, journalism, and biography," which aspire to "absolute compatibility with reality" (ibid., 33). "Paradoxically," however, as Ryan states in another essay, "the reality of which we are native is the least amenable to immersive narration" and, thus, is not a good example of narrative recentering ("Immersion vs. Interactivity"). Though she makes this statement in passing, one assumes that accurate nonfiction is not immersive because the reader already resides in the textual actual world it describes and therefore cannot be transported to it by recentering.

43. Tom Wolfe, *The New Journalism: With an Anthology Edited by Tom Wolfe and E. W. Johnson* (New York: Harper & Row, 1973), 34.

44. John Hellmann, *Fables of Fact: The New Journalism as New Fiction* (Urbana: University of Illinois Press, 1981), 1.

45. Wolfe, *New Journalism*, 34.

46. Though Wolfe doesn't talk about immersion here, it does come up as he discusses the merits of a realist aesthetic: "The most gifted writers are those who manipulate the memory sets of readers in such a rich fashion that they create within the mind of the reader an entire world that resonates with the reader's own real emotions. The events are merely taking place on the page, in print, but the emotions are real. Hence the feeling when one is 'absorbed' in a certain book, 'lost' in it" (ibid., 48). For Ryan as well, immersion involves affective investment, as our tendency to empathize with characters lends them a degree of "pseudoreality" (*Possible Worlds*, 21). She in fact devotes a whole section of *Narrative as Virtual Reality* to "emotional immersion" (148–57). For Wolfe, however, immersion is primarily an affective experience rather than an experience of an alternate ontology.

47. N. Katherine Hayles, *How We Became Posthuman: Virtual Bodies in Cybernetics, Literature, and Informatics* (Chicago: University of Chicago Press, 1999), 196. Hayles carefully distinguishes "the body" or the experience of having a body from "embodiment," because the former has been too easily generalized, normalized, and reified. In this age of informatic technologies "someone's particular experience of embodiment" can easily be converted from the "heterogeneous flux of perception into a reified stable object." Hayles points to positron-emissions tomography (PET) as an example of a contemporary technology that translates individual embodiment into a body by averaging data points "to give an idealized version of the object in question." We have seen this also in first-generation VR's dream of a "natural language of the body," which would eliminate the "noise of difference" generated by the particularities and idiosyncrasies of individual bodies in order to facilitate seamless interaction with a machine. To avoid this body-centric generalization, Hayles conceives of embodiment as singular and momentary instantiation: "Whereas the body can disappear into information

with scarcely a murmur of protest, embodiment cannot, for it is tied to the circumstances of the occasion and the person" (197). The body can be averaged and, thereby, dematerialized and codified; embodiment, on the other hand, describes a particular body, on a particular occasion of having or using that body. Embodiment therefore is less about sensory input, be they media-generated or not, and more about contextualized enactment.

48. Ibid., 53–54.

49. Hayles refers to texts that support or facilitate this kind of engagement as "technotexts": "When a literary work interrogates the inscription technology that produces it, it mobilizes reflexive feedback loops between its imaginative world and the material apparatus embodying that creation as a physical presence." See *Writing Machines* (Cambridge, Mass.: MIT Press, 2002), 25.

50. Hayles, *How We Became Posthuman*, 19.

2. Reading *In Cold Blood* Today

1. Truman Capote, *In Cold Blood* (1966; repr., New York: Vintage, 1994); Marie-Laure Ryan, *Possible Worlds, Artificial Intelligence, and Narrative Theory* (Bloomington: Indiana University Press, 1992), 33.

2. George Plimpton, "The Story behind a Nonfiction Novel," *New York Times*, January 16, 1966, http://www.nytimes.com/books/97/12/28/home/capote-interview .html.

3. A notable example, appearing just a year after the initial publication of *In Cold Blood*, is Phillip Tompkins, "In Cold Fact," *Esquire* 65, no. 6 (1966): 125–71. Tompkins, for the most part, uncovered minor inaccuracies, which he argued suggest larger questions about poetic license in objective journalism. Some of these inaccuracies, though, came at intimate and dramatic moments, suggesting Capote may have played loose with the facts for effect. For example, the last words of one of the killers, Perry Smith, in *In Cold Blood* were "But I do. I apologize." In Tompkins's interviews with Bill Brown, editor of the *Garden City Telegram*, who stood just feet from Smith when he spoke his last words and took notes for his own article on the execution, did not remember an apology. Ronald Weber observes that Tompkins's central criticism of Capote was in his sympathetic portrait of Perry, whom Tompkins saw as an "obscene, semiliterate and cold-blooded killer." See *The Literature of Fact: Literary Nonfiction in American Writing* (Athens: Ohio University Press, 1980), 74. Weber goes on to comment on the significance of this alteration: "Such inaccuracy, if it exists, is of course devastating. If Capote has distorted Perry's character, the book is fatally weakened as a 'true account.' But most readers know nothing of the Clutter murders [described in the book] beyond what Capote relates and so are in no position to measure the book as Tompkins does. Even if they could, such detective work might seem of small importance for the book patently reaches beyond its factual grounding to grasp the reader in the manner of the

novel. It seeks to be, finally, a work of the literary imagination, and it is on this level that the reader can best measure it."

4. Plimpton, "Story behind a Nonfiction Novel."

5. Tom Wolfe, *The New Journalism: With an Anthology Edited by Tom Wolfe and E. W. Johnson* (New York: Harper & Row, 1973), 11.

6. John Hellmann, *Fables of Fact: The New Journalism as New Fiction* (Urbana: University of Illinois Press, 1981), 19.

7. Wolfe, *New Journalism*, 34.

8. Phyllis Frus, *The Politics and Poetics of Journalistic Narrative: The Timely and the Timeless* (Cambridge, U.K.: Cambridge University Press, 1994), 182.

9. Linda Hutcheon, *Narcissistic Narrative: The Metafictional Paradox* (Waterloo, Ont.: Wilfrid Laurier University Press, 1980), 141; Ryan, "Immersion vs. Interactivity: Virtual Reality and Literary Theory," *Postmodern Culture* 5, no. 1 (1994): http://muse .jhu.edu/article/27495.

10. Capote, *In Cold Blood*, 50. All subsequent quotations from *In Cold Blood* will be cited parenthetically in the text.

11. See note 3 above.

12. *In Cold Blood* is a particularly significant novel for law and literature studies. For a survey of relevant contexts, see David Caudill, "The Year of Truman Capote: Legal Ethics and *In Cold Blood*," *Oregon Law Review* 86, no. 2 (2007): 295–328.

13. N. Katherine Hayles, *How We Became Posthuman: Virtual Bodies in Cybernetics, Literature, and Informatics* (Chicago: University of Chicago Press, 1999), 19.

14. Ibid., 196.

3. Incomplete Worlds

1. The advertisement, which ran on television in 1996, can be found on YouTube, uploaded by "DigThatBoxRETRO," as "Super Mario 64 TV Commercial (1996)— Nintendo 64," 2014, http://youtu.be/S4ofBi65U8c.

2. Though *Super Mario 64* was not the first three-dimensional console game, or even the first for Nintendo (Nintendo EAD, *Star Fox* [Nintendo, 1993]), it is commonly recognized as initiating the 3D era.

3. According to the instruction manual included with the game, the user is "not just the player, but the cinematographer, too!" (20). Even though the manual makes a point of alerting users that "one of the tricks to this game is to use the camera skillfully," camera operation is separated out from play.

4. Jesper Juul, *Half-Real: Video Games between Real Rules and Fictional Worlds* (Cambridge, Mass.: MIT Press, 2005), 122.

5. Ibid., 123.

6. Ibid., 138. In this quotation Juul refers to Nintendo EAD, *Super Mario Sunshine* (Nintendo, 2002), but the point is the same.

NOTES TO CHAPTER 3

7. N. Katherine Hayles, *How We Became Posthuman: Virtual Bodies in Cybernetics, Literature, and Informatics* (Chicago: University of Chicago Press, 1999), 19.

8. Katie Salen and Eric Zimmerman, *Rules of Play: Game Design Fundamentals* (Cambridge, Mass.: MIT Press, 2003), 450. As an example, Salen and Zimmerman include as an epigraph the following quotation from François-Dominic Laramée: "All forms of entertainment strive to create suspension of disbelief, a state in which the player's mind forgets that it is being subjected to entertainment and instead accepts what it perceives as reality."

9. Juul, *Half-Real*, 193.

10. Issues with the holodeck typically do not involve the failure to distinguish holodeck simulations from reality. More often technical malfunctions result in an inability to turn the simulations off or the simulations learning they were simulations. A prominent example of both is the episode "Elementary, Dear Data," *Star Trek: The Next Generation*, December 5, 1988.

11. *Game Studies*—described by founding editor Espen Aarseth as "the first academic, peer-reviewed journal dedicated to computer game studies"—posted its inaugural issue in July 2001, just a few months before the terrorist attacks of September 11, a landmark event commonly taken as the end of the dot-com era. See "Computer Game Studies, Year One," *Game Studies* 1, no. 1 (2001): http://www.gamestudies.org/0101/editorial.html.

12. Steven E. Jones, *The Meaning of Video Games: Gaming and Textual Strategies* (New York: Routledge, 2008), 5.

13. Edward Castronova, *Exodus to the Virtual World: How Online Fun Is Changing Reality* (New York: Palgrave Macmillan, 2007).

14. Graham Harman, "On the Undermining of Objects: Grant, Bruno, and Radical Philosophy," in *The Speculative Turn: Continental Materialism and Realism*, ed. Levi R. Bryant, Nick Srnicek, and Graham Harman (Melbourne: re.press, 2011), 25.

15. Levi Bryant, "Flat Ontology," *Larval Subjects*, February 24, 2010, http://larvalsubjects.wordpress.com/2010/02/24/flat-ontology-2/.

16. Both Johan Huizinga's theory of the magic circle (*Homo Ludens* [Boston: Beacon Press, 1955]) and Roger Caillois's discussion of reality versus make-believe (*Man, Play, and Games*, trans. Meyer Barash [1958; repr., Urbana: University of Illinois Press, 2001]) separate play from everyday life. Alexander Galloway traces the ontological divide in the study of videogames even further, back to the ancient Greeks ("Philosophy and Games," audio recording, NYU Game Center Lecture Series, 2009–10, http://gamecenter.nyu.edu/nyu-game-center-lecture-series-philosophy-and-games/).

17. Ian Bogost, "Videogames Are a Mess," address delivered at the annual conference of the Digital Games Research Association, Uxbridge, U.K., September 1–4, 2009, http://www.bogost.com/writing/videogames_are_a_mess.shtml.

18. Juul, *Half-Real*, 1.

19. Ibid., 2.

20. Bogost, "Videogames Are a Mess."

21. Alexander Galloway, *Gaming: Essays on Algorithmic Culture* (Minneapolis: University of Minnesota Press, 2006), 5, 105.

22. See Nick Montfort and Ian Bogost, *Racing the Beam: The Atari Video Computer System* (Cambridge, Mass.: MIT Press, 2009), 146, in which they describe five levels of digital media, situated in context.

23. See Michael Nitsche, *Video Game Spaces: Image, Play, and Structure in 3D Game Worlds* (Cambridge, Mass.: MIT Press, 2008), 15, for his five conceptual planes of gaming.

24. For a concise definition of "flat ontology" see Bryant, "Flat Ontology."

25. See, for example, Astrid Ensslin, *Literary Gaming* (Cambridge, Mass.: MIT Press, 2014), which has little to say about the fictional or virtual and defines literariness as "the sense of linguistic foregrounding" such that "human language (spoken or written) plays a significant aesthetic role" (2). Even in Bogost and Montfort's formulation of the multiple levels that constitute a game (*Racing the Beam*, 145–47), narrative belongs, as it did in later ludologist perspectives, to the formal level and fiction to the reception level.

26. Juul, *Half-Real*, 193.

27. Jim Bizzocchi, "Games and Narrative: An Analytical Framework," *Loading...* 1, no. 1 (2007): http://journals.sfu.ca/loading/index.php/loading/article/viewArticle/1. Bizzocchi suggests that during the ludologist moment, narrative was discussed in very limiting terms. Most often, he explains, use of the term "narrative" is shorthand for "narrative arc," or the sequence of events making up the plot, traditionally including "setup, development, resolution, and denouement." While tight control of a narrative arc has worked well in other media like film and novel, games, because they solicit player interaction, lose "a critical degree of fine authorial control" required for "channeling and guiding the reader's experience of the story" through these traditional devices. As a result, Bizzocchi argues, game narratives should not be expected to fulfill a regular narrative arc. Instead, game scholars should look to other aspects of narrative—such as storyworld, character, emotion, narrative interface, and micronarrative—to discover the real impact of story on gameplay. More recently, Edward Wesp has noted how Juul's model of incomplete worlds forecloses gaming's relationship to more complicated narrative structures, such as the seriality typical of television series. See "A Too-Coherent World: Game Studies and the Myth of 'Narrative' Media," *Game Studies* 14, no. 2 (2014): http://gamestudies.org/1402/articles/wesp.

28. Juul, *Half-Real*, 200.

29. The typical characterization of linear narrative is particularly surprising given the apparent influence of hypertext theory on the early discussion of videogame

narratives. Many objected to in-game narratives for political reasons, arguing that scripted, deterministic structuring limits the freedom of play. Cutscenes became the enemy because they interrupt play, taking agency from the player while defining the player's role without the player's input. Alternately, sandbox games, like DMA Design's *Grand Theft Auto III* (Rockstar Games, 2001) were praised as a "grand anti-authoritarian laboratory" for allowing players to play freely, without having to follow linear path through a set-order narrative (Kevin Parker, "Free Play," *Reason*, April 2004, http://reason.com/archives/2004/04/01/free-play). The same adulation was given to hypertext fiction in the early 1990s by George Landow and others. Landow claimed that hypertext fiction exemplifies Roland Barthes's "writerly text," by presenting nonlinear narratives that elicit reader participation in the ordering of lexia (*Hypertext: The Convergence of Contemporary Critical Theory and Technology* [Baltimore: Johns Hopkins University Press, 1991], 5–6). Even as Espen Aarseth rejected the idea that hypertext positions readers as "co-authors" of the narrative, he never opposed their characterization as nonlinear and described them as requiring "non-trivial" interventions on the part of the reader (*Cybertext: Perspectives on Ergodic Literature* [Baltimore: Johns Hopkins University Press, 1997], 1).

30. Salen and Zimmerman, *Rules of Play*, 449.

31. Juul, *Half-Real*, 132. Though Juul theorizes that there may be games with coherent game worlds, he does not provide any examples or explain what they look like. In his only mention of coherent-world games he states, "Some games contain coherent worlds, where nothing prevents us from imagining them in detail. Most adventure games fall in this category."

32. Ted Friedman, "Making Sense of Software: Computer Games and Interactive Textuality," in *CyberSociety: Computer-Mediated Communication and Community*, ed. Steven G. Jones (Thousand Oaks, Calif.: Sage, 1995), 73–89.

33. For examples, see Espen Aarseth, "Genre Trouble," *Electronic Book Review*, July 26, 2005, http://www.electronicbookreview.com/thread/firstperson/vigilant; Marie-Laure Ryan, *Narrative as Virtual Reality: Immersion and Interactivity in Literature and Electronic Media* (Baltimore: Johns Hopkins University Press, 2003); Bizzocchi, "Games and Narrative"; Richard Walsh, "Emergent Narrative in Interactive Media," *Narrative* 19, no. 1 (2011): 72–85; Ensslin, *Literary Gaming*.

34. Linda Hutcheon, *Narcissistic Narrative: The Metafictional Paradox* (Waterloo, Ont.: Wilfrid Laurier University Press, 1980), 5.

35. Salen and Zimmerman, *Rules of Play*, 455.

4. Gaming in Context

1. Jesper Juul, *Half-Real: Video Games between Real Rules and Fictional Worlds* (Cambridge, Mass.: MIT Press, 2005), 123.

2. Nick Montfort and Ian Bogost, *Racing the Beam: The Atari Video Computer System* (Cambridge, Mass.: MIT Press, 2009). Nolan Bushnell, founder of Atari, had worked as a carnival barker before entering the games industry. Bogost and Montfort suggest that "his contributions to video games owe much to the principles he learned from his experiences at the carnival" (6). They go on to argue that arcade games have more in common with midway games than slot machines, which also have a pay-to-play structure.

3. Montfort and Bogost, *Racing the Beam*, 113.

4. I am borrowing "non-diegetic" from Alexander Galloway's discussion of gamic actions in *Gaming: Essays on Algorithmic Culture* (Minneapolis: University of Minnesota Press, 2006). Galloway adopts the term "non-diegetic" from film studies to describe those game events that cannot be explained by the game world. Non-diegetic actions come in two varieties: player actions, such as configuring options or interacting with a menu, and machine actions, such as power-ups and game-over operations. Whereas Juul points to non-diegetic elements as evidence of the rules showing through the narrative, Galloway insists that these elements cannot be so easily divided because they often intersect or overlap with diegetic elements. As a result, he argues, "video games are complex, active media that may involve both humans and computers and may transpire both inside diegetic space and outside diegetic space" (37).

5. Jason Rhody, "Error, Interface, and the Myth of Immersion," *Electronic Book Review*, March 18, 2008, http://www.electronicbookreview.com/thread/firstperson/poprip.

6. See Michel Foucault, "What Is an Author?" in *Aesthetics, Method, and Epistemology*, vol. 2 of *Essential Works of Foucault, 1954–1984* (New York: New Press, 1969), 205–22.

7. Walter J. Ong, *Orality and Literacy: The Technologizing of the Word* (New York: Routledge, 1982), 39.

8. Thomas Davenport and John Beck, *The Attention Economy: Understanding the New Currency of Business* (Cambridge, Mass.: Harvard Business Review Press, 2002).

9. Videos demonstrating these player-directed effects can be found all over YouTube. For example, "jamescorock" has posted several in which he describes his reaction to seeing the effects for the first time. In his video "Walkthrough for Eternal Darkness—How to Get Mantorok's Alignment" (August 2, 2009, http://youtu.be/yk kHaoNXbCE) he encounters the deleted-saves sanity effect and exclaims, "This is the worst thing you can do to a videogame nerd like me" (2:11).

10. When jamescorock gets the "blue screen of death" effect, he explains that it prompted him to submit his GameCube console to the Nintendo repair center (3:25).

11. The implications of this sanity effect stretch even further into the business and politics of game development. After losing a lawsuit to Epic Games in 2012, Silicon

Knights had to cancel their much-anticipated sequel to *Eternal Darkness*. Denis Dyack then left to start Precursor Games, while Nintendo retained ownership of the *Eternal Darkness* title. See Brian Sipple, "'Too Human 2' & '3,' 'Eternal Darkness 2' among Silicon Knights Cancellation Graveyard," *Game Rant*, December 12, 2012, http://gamer ant.com/too-human-2-3-cancelled-screens/; Brian Crecente, "Silicon Knights Unloads Property, Closes Office, Continues Battle with Epic Games," *Polygon*, May 9, 2013, http://www.polygon.com/2013/5/9/4316936/silicon-knights-epic-games-precursor -games.

12. *Eternal Darkness* presents a complicated metaphysics of time and intriguing theorization of immersion; unfortunately there is not space to deal with it adequately here.

13. *.hack* is a massive transmedia franchise involving games, anime movies, novels, manga, and toys. For simplicity's sake, I will address only *Infection*, though much of the argument will apply to the series as a whole.

14. Koichi Mashimo and Masayuki Yoshihara, *.hack//Liminality, Vol. 1: In the Case of Mai Minase*, DVD (Bee Train and Bandai Games, 2002). This DVD packaged with *Infection* depicts players of *The World* using a joystick that resembles a white PlayStation2 controller. Though there is no reference to or appearance of the controllers in the game—obviously—the broader media ecology further represents the player's engagement with the gaming apparatus as a part of the fiction.

15. This is in contrast to games like *Assassin's Creed* (Ubisoft, 2007). In *Assassin's Creed* players do not take the role of assassin directly, but rather the role of the assassins' descendent Desmond Miles, who reenacts his assassin ancestors' lives with the aid of the Animus, a VR machine that generates historically accurate simulations by tapping into the user's DNA memory. When Desmond is not in the Animus and so no longer mediating interaction with the assassin simulation, the player takes Desmond as an avatar.

16. Samuel Axon, "PlayStation Network Down [PSN]," *Mashable*, February 28, 2010, http://mashable.com/2010/02/28/psn-down-8001050f/.

17. Gregg Keizer, "Windows Market Share Dives below 90% for First Time," *Computerworld*, December 1, 2008, http://www.computerworld.com/s/article/9121938/ Windows_market_share_dives_below_90_for_first_time. At time of writing, Windows constitutes a little over 83 percent of desktop operating systems globally according to *StatCounter* ("Top 7 Desktop OSs on Apr 2016," May 6, 2016, http://gs.stat counter.com/#desktop-os-ww-monthly-201604-201604-bar). If one considers desktop and mobile operating systems, Windows was third in percentage of devices shipped in 2015 with 11.7 percent behind Apple's iOS and OS X at a combined 12.28 percent and Google Android's 53 percent (Keizer, "Windows Comes Up Third in OS Clash Two Years Early," *Computerworld*, April 1, 2016, http://www.computerworld.com/article/

3050931/microsoft-windows/windows-comes-up-third-in-os-clash-two-years-early
.html).

18. Paul Virilio, *Speed and Politics*, trans. Mark Polizzotti (New York: Semiotext[e],
1986).

19. Marc Ambinder, "U.S. to Be Hit by Massive Cyber Attack on Feb. 16. Asterisk,"
The Atlantic, February 10, 2010, http://www.theatlantic.com/politics/archive/2010/
02/us-to-be-hit-by-massive-cyber-attack-on-feb-16-asterisk/35708/.

20. Yaakov Lappin, "Israel, Iran Wage Cyber Warfare in the Battlefield of the Future,"
Jerusalem Post, May 30, 2014, http://www.jpost.com/Defense/Israel-and-Iran-wage-
cyber-warfare-in-the-battlefield-of-the-future-354872.

21. As Miguel Sicart puts it in *The Ethics of Computer Games* (Cambridge, Mass.:
MIT Press, 2009), "Players and player communities are cultural and embodied outside the game experience, where other values that are not those of the game as object,
the player, or the player community are dominant" (120). Sicart explains that even if
alone and offline, players enter into a network of "distributed responsibility" connecting players to developers, community, and culture that made the game. He emphasizes
that this occurs through the fiction as a medium of informational exchange.

22. Edward Castronova, *Synthetic Worlds: The Business and Culture of Online Games*
(Chicago: University of Chicago Press, 2005).

23. Constance Steinkuehler, "The Mangle of Play," *Games and Culture: A Journal of
Interactive Media* 1, no. 3 (2006): 199–213.

24. Ian Bogost, "Videogames Are a Mess," address delivered at the annual conference of the Digital Games Research Association, Uxbridge, U.K., September 1–4,
2009; Linda Hutcheon, *Narcissistic Narrative: The Metafictional Paradox* (Waterloo,
Ont.: Wilfrid Laurier University Press, 1980), 5.

5. Metafiction and the Perils of Ubiquitous Mediation

1. Mark B. N. Hansen, *Bodies in Code: Interfaces with Digital Media* (New York:
Routledge, 2006), 2.

2. Ibid., 5.

3. Ibid., 2.

4. Machiko Kusahara, "Mini-Screens and Big Screens: Aspects of Mixed Reality
in Everyday Life," in *Cast01: Living in Mixed Realities* (Bonn, Deu.: netzspannugn.org,
2001), 31, http://netzspannung.org/version1/extensions/cast01-proceedings/pdf/cast
01_proceedings.pdf.

5. Hansen, *Bodies in Code*, 5.

6. Kusahara, "Mini-Screens and Big Screens," 31.

7. Patricia Waugh, *Metafiction: The Theory and Practice of Self-Conscious Fiction*
(New York: Methuen, 1984), 40.

8. Brian McHale, in *Postmodernist Fiction* (New York: Methuen, 1987), calls the play with ontological boundaries the defining feature of postmodern literature. At the same time, numerous fields of research and cultural production were experimenting with the capacity of media to manipulate such boundaries. While there is not space here to pursue the idea, one could suggest that postmodern fiction anticipates digital technologies in much the same way that, as Peter Galassi has shown in *Before Photography: Painting and the Invention of Photography* (New York: Museum of Modern Art, 1981), certain painterly styles in the early nineteenth century anticipated photography.

9. Linda Hutcheon, *Narcissistic Narrative: The Metafictional Paradox* (Waterloo, Ont.: Wilfrid Laurier University Press, 1980), 3. Hutcheon identifies this position with Gerald Graff, naming him as exemplary of attitudes toward narcissistic narratives. Both McHale (*Postmodernist Fiction*) and Waugh (*Metafiction*) also identify this critical reaction to postmodern fiction and attempt to address concerns that metafictional reference breaks the life–art binary by explaining these techniques as reshaping realism.

10. Marie-Laure Ryan, "Immersion vs. Interactivity: Virtual Reality and Literary Theory," *Postmodern Culture* 5, no. 1 (1994): http://muse.jhu.edu/journals/postmodern_culture/v005/5.1ryan.html.

11. Hutcheon, *Narcissistic Narrative*, 3.

12. Ibid., 5.

13. The reference to the "nontrivial effort" of reading a text is derived from Espen J. Aarseth, *Cybertext: Perspectives on Ergodic Literature* (Baltimore: Johns Hopkins University Press, 1997), 1. Though most frequently associated with electronic texts, Aarseth found numerous examples of ergodic texts in print literature: "The variety and ingenuity of devices used in these texts demonstrate that paper can hold its own against the computer as a technology of ergodic texts" (10).

14. Kusahara, "Mini-Screens and Big Screens," 33.

15. Ibid., 31.

16. See Mark Nunes, *Cyberspaces of Everyday Life* (Minneapolis: University of Minnesota Press, 2006).

17. Edward Castronova, *Synthetic Worlds: The Business and Culture of Online Games* (Chicago: University of Chicago Press, 2005), 159.

18. Hansen, *Bodies in Code*, 5.

19. Ibid., 2.

20. Kusahara, "Mini-Screens and Big Screens," 31.

21. David Foster Wallace, "E Unibus Pluram: Television and U.S. Fiction," *Review of Contemporary Fiction* 13, no. 2 (1993): 172. All subsequent quotations from "E Unibus Pluram" will be cited parenthetically in the text.

22. Qtd. in ibid., although Wallace doesn't cite his source.

23. This scene occurs in "Somebody to Love," *30 Rock*, November 15, 2007. For a discussion, see Rosario Santiago, "'30 Rock' and Verizon Strike Unconventional Advertising Deal," *BuddyTV*, December 3, 2007, http://www.buddytv.com/articles/30-rock/30-rock-and-verizon-strike-unc-14333.aspx.

24. See Slavoj Žižek, *The Sublime Object of Ideology* (New York: Verso, 1989), 18 and elsewhere.

25. See Adam Kelly, "David Foster Wallace and the New Sincerity in American Fiction," in *Consider David Foster Wallace: Critical Essays*, ed. David Hering (Los Angeles: SSMG Press, 2010), 131–46.

26. Jay David Bolter, *Writing Space: The Computer, Hypertext, and the History of Writing* (Hillsdale, N.J.: Lawrence Erlbaum Associates, 1991), 155.

6. When What's Real Doesn't Matter

1. Mark Z. Danielewski, *House of Leaves* (New York: Pantheon Books, 2000). All subsequent quotations from *House of Leaves* will be cited parenthetically in the text.

2. Jon Thiem, "Textualization of the Reader," in *Magical Realism: Theory, History, Community*, ed. Lois Parkinson Zamora and Wendy B. Faris (Durham, N.C.: Duke University Press, 1995), 236.

3. Ibid., 240.

4. Ibid., 241; Wolfgang Iser, "The Reality of Fiction: A Functionalist Approach to Literature," *New Literary History* 7, no. 1 (1975): 7.

5. Iser, "Reality of Fiction," 20.

6. See, for example, Thomas Pavel, *Fictional Worlds* (Cambridge, Mass.: Harvard University Press, 1986).

7. Iser, "Reality of Fiction," 20.

8. Jessica Pressman, "*House of Leaves*: Reading the Networked Novel," *Studies in American Fiction* 34, no. 1 (2006): 107–28; Mark B. N. Hansen, *Bodies in Code: Interfaces with Digital Media* (New York: Routledge, 2006), 222.

9. N. Katherine Hayles, *Electronic Literature: New Horizons for the Literary* (South Bend, Ind.: University of Notre Dame Press, 2008), 177. Hayles argues that novels like *House of Leaves* that were arranged and printed as digital files, as opposed to using analog-layout methods, qualify as electronic literature. Complicating this issue somewhat, Danielewski claims to have composed the novel—layout and all—with pencil and paper, only learning to arrange it digitally afterward to prepare it for publication.

10. Iser, "Reality of Fiction," 20.

11. Linda Hutcheon, *Narcissistic Narrative: The Metafictional Paradox* (Waterloo, Ont.: Wilfrid Laurier University Press, 1980), 5.

12. For examples, see Hayles "The Future of Literature: Print Novels and the Mark of the Digital," in *Electronic Literature*; Hansen "The Digital Topography of Mark Z. Danielewski's *House of Leaves*," in *Bodies in Code*; and Pressman "*House of Leaves*."

13. Hansen, *Bodies in Code*, 225.

14. An adequate description of what Truant experienced would have been quite difficult, as it is specifically and importantly olfactory in origin. Throughout the narrative, the influence of *The Navidson Record* on its caretakers is manifested through smell. Zampanò found the odor so offensive he sealed his apartment. When Truant first enters Zampanò's place, he notes, "What hit me first was the smell" (xv). He explains how the "extremely layered" odor had at first "overwhelmed" him but, after his time with Zampanò's notes, he "can no longer remember the smell only my reaction to it" (xvi). When Truant notes that his panic attack in the alley was triggered by "the scent of something bitter & foul," he links this event to his work on *The Navidson Record* (26n33). Recognizing that what he calls "the language of nausea" is not and can never be the reader's experience of the language of the book, he forgoes attempting to describe what paranoia smells like. Instead he leads the reader through an exercise to elicit a corresponding experience of reading.

15. Pressman, *"House of Leaves,"* 112.

16. N. Katherine Hayles, *Writing Machines* (Cambridge, Mass.: MIT Press, 2002), 123.

17. On the first page without a blue box (146) Zampanò cites W. J. T. Mitchell citing Roland Barthes's "The Reality Effect," which argues that seemingly superfluous details in a work of literature suggest that "this is indeed an unfiltered sample of the real." These are the citations he provides: "Roland Barthes' 'The Reality Effect,' in *French Literary Theory Today*, ed. Tzvetan Todorov (Cambridge: Cambridge University Press, 1982), p. 11–17" (146n191) and "William J. Mitchell's *The Reconfigured Eye: Visual Truth In The Post-Photographic Era* (Cambridge, Massachusetts: The MIT Press, 1994), p. 27" (146n192).

18. The appearance of just the two words, "two frames," with a large space between them, solidifies the association between words and film frames as discrete units of recording. This layout, two words at the extreme margins of the page, was established at the beginning of the sentence. "A life" appears in the extreme left of 197 and "time" on 198 at the extreme right. On 199, "finished" and "between" now share the same page though pinned to the margins. The words on 200, "in the space of," appear normally spaced in the exact middle of the line. This places the phrase in the distance between "finished" and "between," which are still visible through the printed page, and "two" and "frames" on the following page. In this respect, "in the space of" names the location where a "lifetime" is "finished": between "two frames" in the film, this white space between words in the book. It is another example of how the novel enacts what is being described for the reader by means of the printed page.

19. Lev Manovich, *The Language of New Media* (Cambridge, Mass.: MIT Press, 2002), 29.

20. Ibid., 28; Roland Barthes, *Elements of Semiology*, trans. Annette Lavers and Colin Smith (New York: Hill and Wang, 1968), 64.

21. For pages 202 to 205, across which the sentence about the "dark line" appears, the layout changes slightly to emphasize the "dark line" of the text. Whereas the isolated line of text from pages 194 to 201 exaggerate the space between words, that spacing is reduced for the "dark line" sentence. Setting four or five words per page retains a sense of the discrete units of language while also making the passage more visibly a dark line.

22. Sinda Gregory and Larry McCaffery, "Haunted House: An Interview with Mark Z. Danielewski," *Critique: Studies in Contemporary Fiction* 44, no. 2 (2003): 121.

23. See Pressman, *"House of Leaves,"* 115.

24. JoeyELP, "Is There *REALLY* Anything to 'Figure Out' about This Book?" *House of Leaves*, October 20, 2008, http://forums.markzdanielewski.com/forum/house-of-leaves/house-of-leaves-aa/5527-is-there-really-anything-to-figure-out-about-this-book. The suggestion that the book ultimately does not answer the puzzles it poses inspired this nine-page forum discussion. Here is how the post originator, JoeyELP, put the issue: "I'm just trying to be honest with myself. I mean, if we have 120,000 posts, 20,000 users, and there's still no definite conclusion who wrote the book, or if some of the main characters even 'exist,' then doesn't occams [*sic*] razor suggest that MZD wrote an ambiguous [*sic*] book and there isn't some final, all-encompassing explanation sitting on MZD's desk? Not to say that certain things can't be discovered, and that its [*sic*] not fun to do so, but come on. Either its [*sic*] too ambiguously [*sic*] written for 20k people to figure out over years, or MZD is very deliberately keeping his devoted fans in the dark. In that vein, I'm beginning to see this book as a Rorschach test, or poetry, rather than a cohesive (ha!) narrative."

25. Will Slocombe, "'This Is Not for You': Nihilism and the House That Jacques Built," *Modern Fiction Studies* 51, no. 1 (2005): 106.

26. David Foster Wallace, "E Unibus Pluram: Television and U.S. Fiction," *Review of Contemporary Fiction* 13, no. 2 (1993): 193.

27. For an extensive discussion of Navidson's reentry into the house as an expression of his feelings of responsibility for and to Delial as the Other, see William Little, "Nothing to Write Home About: Impossible Reception in Mark Z. Danielewski's *House of Leaves*," in *The Mourning After: Attending the Wake of Postmodernism*, ed. Neil Brooks and Josh Toth (New York: Rodopi, 2007), 169–99.

28. Although the novel predates the film, there was also a short documentary about Carter—Dan Krauss, *The Death of Kevin Carter: Casualty of the Bang Bang Club*, DVD (Berkeley: UC Berkeley Graduate School of Journalism, 2005). For more on Carter, see Scott MacLeod, "The Life and Death of Kevin Carter," *Time*, September 12, 1994, http://content.time.com/time/magazine/article/0,9171,981431,00.html.

29. "Pulitzer Prize Winning Photographer Kills Himself and Leaves Suicide Note about World Hunger," *TruthorFiction.com*, August 10, 2005, http://www.truthorfiction .com/rumors/k/kevincarter.htm; Brett M. Christensen, "Kevin Carter Pulitzer Prize Photograph," *Hoax-Slayer*, January 22, 2008, http://www.hoax-slayer.com/kevin-car ter-pulitzer.shtml.

30. Gregory and McCaffery, "Haunted House," 121.

7. Acceptable Losses

1. EDIDDY99, "Are We Ready for Modern Warfare? Terrorism Simulator *Spoil-ers*," *Playstation Show Podcast*, October 28, 2009, http://theplaystationshow.com/ news/are-we-ready-for-modern-warefare-spoilers/; Ludwig Kietzmann, "New Modern Warfare: Airport Murder Simulator 2 Video Game Glorifies Terrorism," *Joystiq*, October 28, 2009, http://www.joystiq.com/2009/10/28/new-modern-warfare-airport -murder-simulator-2-video-game-glorif/.

2. Thor Thorsen, "Russian Media Links Airport Bombing, *Modern Warfare 2*," *Gamespot*, January 25, 2011, http://www.gamespot.com/news/6286915.html.

3. See Ian Bogost, "Why Debates about Video Games Aren't Really about Video Games," *Kotaku*, August 1, 2011, http://kotaku.com/5826559/why-debates-about-video -games-arent-about-video-games.

4. *Brown v. Entertainment Merchants Association*, 564 U.S. 08-1448 (2010), http:// www.supremecourt.gov/oral_arguments/argument_transcripts/08-1448.pdf.

5. See Katie Salen and Eric Zimmerman, *Rules of Play: Game Design Fundamentals* (Cambridge, Mass.: MIT Press, 2003).

6. *Modern Warfare 2* fulfills both of the established forms of realism identified by Alexander Galloway in *Gaming: Essays on Algorithmic Culture* (Minneapolis: University of Minnesota Press, 2006). Neither model, he points out, adequately addresses the ways videogames supplement representation with the phenomenon of action. With this in mind, his concept of social realism attempts to read gameplay as an extension of the player's lived social life. Rather than focusing on a game's verisimilitude or potential influence on players, Galloway describes the relationship between on-screen and off-screen environments as one of "correspondence," a two-way exchange where the affordances within the game world speak to and respond to the player's experiences in the real world (72). Social realism thereby posits a relationship between the virtual and the actual hinged on the real activity of playing the game. Unfortunately, Galloway's formulation winds up focusing on ideology over mechanics. For example, comparing the Syrian game *Under Ash* by Syrian developer Dar Al-Fikr (2001) to *America's Army*, developed by the U.S. Army (2002), he writes, "The engine is the same, but the narrative is different" (82). As a result, his model of social realism returns to representation, even as it posits a need to account for action. My concept of mixed realism,

which owes much to Galloway's work, hinges on returning to gamic action, which functions as the crease point where the player's lived environment folds back on and becomes the context for play in a virtual environment.

7. Slavoj Žižek, *The Fragile Absolute; or, Why Is the Christian Legacy Worth Fighting For?* (New York: Verso, 2001), 77.

8. Philip Alston and United Nations Human Rights Council, *Report of the Special Rapporteur on Extrajudicial, Summary, or Arbitrary Executions, with Addendum: Study on Targeted Killings* (Geneva: United Nations, 2010), http://www2.ohchr.org/english/bodies/hrcouncil/docs/14session/A.HRC.14.24.Add6.pdf.

9. Konami's *Metal Gear* franchise in particular confronts players with their position in the military-entertainment complex through innovative use of the medium and intelligent self-reference. See Tanner Higgins, "'Turn the Game Console Off Right Now!': War, Subjectivity , and Control in *Metal Gear Solid 2*," in *Joystick Soldiers: The Politics of Play in Military Video Games*, ed. Nina Huntemann and Matthew Thomas Payne (New York: Routledge), 252–71; and James Paul Gee, "Playing *Metal Gear Solid 4* Well: Being a Good Snake," in *Well Played 1.0: Video Games, Value and Meaning* (Pittsburgh, Pa.: ETC Press, 2009), http://www.etc.cmu.edu/etcpress/node/284.

10. Galloway, *Gaming*, 78.

11. Ed Halter, *From Sun Tzu to Xbox: War and Video Games* (New York: Thunder's Mouth Press, 2006), 146.

12. Bruce Sterling, "War Is Virtual Hell," *Wired*, April 1993, http://www.wired.com/wired/archive/1.01/virthell_pr.html; Tim Lenoir, "All but War Is Simulation: The Military-Entertainment Complex," *Configurations* 8, no. 3 (2000): 289–335; James Der Derian, *Virtuous War: Mapping the Military-Industrial-Media-Entertainment Network* (Boulder, Colo.: Westview Press, 2001); McKenzie Wark, *Gamer Theory* (Cambridge, Mass.: Harvard University Press, 2007); Halter, *From Sun Tzu to Xbox*.

13. David Hambling, "Game Controllers Driving Drones, Nukes," *Wired*, April 19, 2008, http://www.wired.com/dangerroom/2008/07/wargames/.

14. See Der Derian, *Virtuous War*.

15. John Arquilla and David Ronfeldt, "Fight Networks with Networks," *Full Alert: An Arsenal of Ideas for the War against Terrorism*, Fall 2001, http://www.rand.org/pubs/periodicals/rand-review/issues/rr-12-01/fullalert.html. Arquilla and Ronfeldt do not mention videogames specifically; however, because games are examples of advanced U.S. military technologies covered in typically pro-Western narratives, they would seem to fulfill both advantages the United States can claim in network-versus-network conflict.

16. Halter, *From Sun Tzu to Xbox*, 153.

17. Ibid., 165.

18. *Marine Doom* came out of the Marine Corps Modeling and Simulation Management Office's Personal Computer–Based Wargames Catalog, a survey of over thirty

military-themed commercial games with the intent to "determine if any have the potential to teach a better appreciation for the art and science of war straight out of the box, with no modifications required" (qtd. in ibid., 166). The vast majority of games they cataloged were "little more than electronically enhanced versions of old tabletop war games," which were best "suited for learning command-level strategy or air defense" (167). The only game the catalog saw as having any potential was id Software's *Doom II* (GT Interactive, 1994). Lieutenants Dan Snyder and Scott Barnett created *Marine Doom* through the standard "modding" practice of developing a WAD, a package file that replaces in-game graphics and level designs, to turn the alien monsters roaming a mazelike dungeon into uniformed soldiers on a dusty, barbwired battlefield.

19. Qtd. in ibid., 196–97.

20. "AAA" designation refers to videogames with excellent production value and the expectation of broad marketability and high sales. AAA games are counted on to be major and significant releases. Many AAA military shooters, like the Zipper Interactive's *SOCOM: U.S. Navy SEALs* (Sony Computer Entertainment, 2002), stand as their own version of spectacular, cinematic warfare and have little connection to actual combat scenarios or tactics. There are, however, several games, like *Full Spectrum Warrior*, that do attempt to replicate real military tactics or, like those developed by Kuma Reality Games, reenact historical battles as playable FPS scenarios. Still, even if they are not interested in simulation, most military shooters will consult with military officials in order to make claims to verisimilitude.

21. Prior to *Call of Duty 4: Modern Warfare*, all *Call of Duty* games were set in World War II.

22. Alexander Galloway and Eugene Thacker, *The Exploit: A Theory of Networks* (Minneapolis: University of Minnesota Press, 2007), 15.

23. Ibid., 6.

24. For recent treatments, see Patrick Crogan, *Gameplay Mode: War, Simulation, and Technoculture* (Minneapolis: University of Minnesota Press, 2011); Nina Huntemann and Matthew Thomas Payne, eds., *Joystick Soldiers: The Politics of Play in Military Video Games* (New York: Routledge, 2010); and Gerald Voorhees, Josh Call, and Katie Whitlock, *Guns, Grenades, and Grunts: First-Person Shooter Games* (New York: Continuum, 2012).

25. Galloway and Thacker, *The Exploit*, 66.

26. Der Derian, *Virtuous War*, xv.

27. Ibid., xvi.

28. Wark, *Gamer Theory*, 10.

29. Alston and United Nations Human Rights Council, *Study on Targeted Killings*, 25.

30. For more on "war porn" websites, see Matthis Chiroux, "Is Our Military Addicted to 'War Porn'?" *Huffington Post*, January 15, 2012, http://www.huffingtonpost.com/matthis-chiroux/is-our-military-addicted-_b_1206537.html.

198 NOTES TO CHAPTER 7

31. In a video titled "!!!READ DESCRIPTION!!! AC-130 Strike" (2007, http://
youtu.be/COBa1fCCW98), user "Pr3d4toR6sic6" dubs the audio from an actual AC-
130 bombing over the video of the "Death from Above" mission. Further solidifying
the comparison, statements made in the selected audio, such as "These guys are going
to town," also appear as lines of dialogue in the Modern Warfare radio chatter.

32. Žižek, Fragile Absolute, 77.

33. Wark, Gamer Theory, 10.

34. Games roughly contemporary with Modern Warfare 2 that include morality
mechanics include Irrational Games' Bioshock (2K Games, 2007), Bethesda Game
Studios' Fallout 3 (Bethesda Softworks, 2008), and BioWare's Mass Effect (Microsoft
Game Studios, 2007), to name only a few.

35. Tom Bissell, "It's a Massacre! The Appalling Failure of Modern Warfare 2's 'No
Russian' Mission," Crispy Gamer, November 13, 2009, http://www.crispygamer.com/
features/2009-11-13/its-a-massacre-the-appalling-failure-of-modern-warfare-2s-no
-russian-mission.asp.

36. Scott Shane, "C.I.A. to Expand Use of Drones in Pakistan," New York Times,
December 4, 2009, http://www.nytimes.com/2009/12/04/world/asia/04drones.html.

37. Noah Shachtman, "Up to 320 Civilians Killed in Pakistan Drone War: Report,"
Wired, October 19, 2009, http://www.wired.com/dangerroom/2009/10/up-to-320
-civilians-killed-in-pakistan-drone-war-report/.

38. New America Foundation, "The Year of the Drone: An Analysis of U.S. Drone
Strikes in Pakistan, 2004–2011," Counterterrorism Strategy Initiative, April 14, 2011,
http://counterterrorism.newamerica.net/drones.

39. Galloway and Thacker, The Exploit, 115.

Coda

1. Hal Foster, The Return of the Real: Art and Theory at the End of the Century
(Cambridge, Mass.: MIT Press, 1996), 132.

2. Ibid., 136, 132.

3. Mark B. N. Hansen, Bodies in Code: Interfaces with Digital Media (New York:
Routledge, 2006), 225.

4. Cormac McCarthy, Blood Meridian: or, The Evening Redness in the West (1985;
repr., New York: Vintage, 2010), 57. All subsequent quotations from Blood Meridian
will be cited parenthetically in the text.

5. Harold Bloom, "Introduction," in Cormac McCarthy, ed. Harold Bloom (New
York: Infobase, 2009), 1–2.

6. Timothy Parrish, "History and the Problem of Evil in McCarthy's Western
Novels," in The Cambridge Companion to Cormac McCarthy, ed. Steven Frye (Cambridge, U.K.: Cambridge University Press, 2013), 76.

7. Ibid., 71.

8. Steven Shaviro, "'The Very Life of the Darkness': A Reading of *Blood Meridian*," in *Cormac McCarthy*, ed. Bloom, 19.

9. Ibid.

10. Ibid., 20.

11. *Brown v. Entertainment Merchants Association*, 564 U.S. 08-1448 (2010), http://www.supremecourt.gov/oral_arguments/argument_transcripts/08-1448.pdf.

12. Shaviro, "Very Life of the Darkness," 18.

13. Parrish, "History and the Problem of Evil in McCarthy's Western Novels," 76.

14. During the revolutionary protests in several Arab countries during the spring of 2010, activists frequently used social media sites like Twitter and Facebook to organize and coordinate their activities. See Gadi Wolfsfeld, Elad Segev, and Tamir Sheafer, "Social Media and the Arab Spring Politics Comes First," *International Journal of Press/Politics* 18, no. 2 (2013): 115–37. The numerous news stories discussing the role of social media in these movements frequently circulated through news aggregating websites like the *Huffington Post*, which were in turn shared by users on social media sites. The phrase "pics or shut the fuck up" frequently appears on such sites—typically abbreviated as "pics or stfu"—by commenters demanding photographs as evidence to support another user's claims. See "pics or stfu," *Urban Dictionary*, December 27, 2003, http://www.urbandictionary.com/define.php?term=pics%20or%20stfu.

15. "Catfishing" is the practice whereby a person fabricates an online identity to lure romantic partners under false pretenses. See "Catfish," *Urban Dictionary*, July 22, 2010, http://www.urbandictionary.com/define.php?term=catfish. The reference here is to the former Notre Dame football player Manti Te'o whose longtime girlfriend turned out to have been invented and impersonated by a family friend, Ronaiah Tuiasosopo. See Erik Brady and Rachel George, "Manti Te'o's 'Catfish' Story Is a Common One," *USA Today*, January 18, 2013, http://www.usatoday.com/story/sports/ncaaf/2013/01/17/manti-teos-catfish-story-common/1566438/. The second reference is to the Invisible Children's *Kony 2012* documentary, which, a few months prior to the Te'o story, sparked controversy over the effectiveness and authenticity of its advocacy. At the time of writing, the film has over ninety-eight million views on YouTube. For a discussion see Ashley Mentzer, "*Kony 2012*: Fake Advocacy?" *Huffington Post*, March 13, 2012, http://www.huffingtonpost.com/the-state-press/kony-2012_b_1339081.html.

16. "Powell: Iraq Hiding Weapons, Aiding Terrorists," *CNN*, February 6, 2003, http://www.cnn.com/2003/US/02/05/sprj.irq.powell.un/.

17. "NSA Taps Data from 9 Major Net Firms," *USA Today*, June 6, 2013, http://www.usatoday.com/story/news/2013/06/06/nsa-surveillance-internet-companies/2398345/.

INDEX

(*continued from page ii*)

TIMOTHY J. WELSH is assistant professor of English at Loyola University New Orleans.